CHARLOTTE'S ST

Pamela Dearlove

CHARLOTTE'S STORY

FROM LIFE AS A CHILD IN WARTIME NAZI GERMANY TO SETTLING IN THE HEMINGFORDS

2024

Copyright © Pamela Dearlove, 2024
All rights reserved

No part of this book may be reproduced, or stored in a retrieval system, or transmitted in any form or by any means, electronic, mechanical, photocopying, recording, or otherwise, without express written permission of the publisher.

Preface

Charlotte's Story arose out of a different WW2 story that I had begun to research. I asked Charlotte if she would translate some diaries written by Alois Neugebauer while he was a German POW, which I had been lent by his family, who did not speak German. Whilst we were working on the diaries, Charlotte found that many memories of her life in Germany kept jumping into her head. These were so interesting that I began to write them down and set them in the context of her life in wartime Europe and peace-time Britain.

Many thanks go to Charlotte, without whose clear and colourful observations this interesting story could not have emerged from a particularly turbulent time in world history. I am grateful to her for helping me to gain some idea of what life was like in Germany at a time when Hitler and the Nazis dominated Europe.

I would also like to thank Charlotte's daughters Susan, Michelle, and Helen for their encouragement and help by searching for photos.

I thank my son Richard for reading the story and inserting the photos into the lengthy text.

But I am especially grateful to David Yeandle for showing me how it was possible for my document named *Charlotte's Story* to be published. He then used his computing skills to help me arrange it in a suitable format for publication as a book.

Contents

Preface	v
Contents	vii
Table of Figures	x
Introduction	1
How Charlotte's Story Came to Be Related	1
Because of Hitler	1
The Nazi Era	2
The Krabbe and Dabelstein Families	5
The Move to Bielefeld	14
Hanover, 1932	16
The Third Reich, 1933	23
Flowers for Hitler, 1934	24
A Wedding in Saxony, 1934	28
Death of Muschi, 1937	31
The 1936 Olympics	33
The Communist Threat, 1936	34
Kristallnacht, 1938	35
Propaganda	36
Re-Education, 1938	39
Hitler Youth, etc.	44
War, 1939	47
Life with Tante Lotti and Onkel Franz	52
Memories of Onkel Franz	56

Life with Tante Leni, 1940/41	62
Conscription, 1941	69
Death of Andreas, 1942	71
Pflicht (Duty) Year at Domäne Dütschow	76
Dütschow, 1942	76
Secretarial College and Tante Leni, 1943	79
Banzin – A New Life, 1943/4	79
Romance, 1943/44	85
Summer 1944	85
Life on the Banzin Farm, 1943–45	88
Jürgen's Death, July 1944	94
Bad News, July 1944	96
October 1944	97
Charlotte's Weekend Breaks	99
A Leap to Save Her Life	99
Blueberry Treat, Summer 1944	101
The Final Solution	102
Burning of Documents	106
Charlotte's Brave or Rash Decision	108
Yalta	115
Good Advice Given?	115
Hitler's Suicide, 30 April 1945	118
Escape	122
The War Is Over	128
A New Way of Life, May 1945	132

Liberators	136
The Officers' Mess	142
On the Buffers	145
Wolfenbüttel, 1945 or 1946	148
Rule-Breaking Trysts	151
Sweden, c. 1946, Aged 19/20	153
A New Start	156
Adapting to Life in England	159
Tante Lotti and Tante Leni in the Soviet Zone	161
Holidays Abroad	162
A Holiday in the Black Forest	164
To Huntingdonshire	165
Daily Life for Charlotte's Aunts under the Soviet Regime	169
Charlotte's Projects	173
Making a Difference	173
Danger in Peacetime	176
Further Projects	177
Visit to Banzin	180
Postwar Eastern Germany	182
The Wartime Romance	183
Enduring Friendships	184

Table of Figures

Figure 1 Theodor Martin Krabbe's grave 6
Figure 2 Stift Bethlehem 7
Figure 3 Theodor Krabbe 8
Figure 4 Andreas Krabbe 10
Figure 5 The Krabbe family, Charlotte 2 months old, 24/8/1926 11
Figure 6 Krabbe Family with Tante Leni, c. 1926/1927 13
Figure 7 Charlotte's sixth birthday at Bielefeld, 1932 14
Figure 8 Jürgen and Charlotte, c. 1931 15
Figure 9 Hildesheimer Straße 118, Hanover 16
Figure 10 Muschi Krabbe, sanatorium at Sülzhayn 17
Figure 11 Christmas in Hanover 19
Figure 12 Christmas with Andreas Krabbe 20
Figure 13 Charlotte, 4, Jürgen, 7 with Andreas and Muschi, Hanover, 1930 21
Figure 14 Jürgen, 6, on his first day at school 22
Figure 15 Children greeting Hitler 26
Figure 16 Muschi in the sanatorium, Sülzhayn 30
Figure 17 Jürgen, Charlotte, and Anneliese Hemmings at Tante Lotti's 32
Figure 18 Charlotte, aged 12 (top row, third from left), school group photo, 1938, class 3a with classmates, including Edith and Merigart 41
Figure 19 School assembly hall 42
Figure 20 Charlotte, 14, class 5a, at school in Hanover, 1940 51
Figure 21 School group photo, class 5a, Hanover, 1940 51
Figure 22 Onkel Franz 56
Figure 23 Ludwigslust postcard 57
Figure 24 Tante Leni with Ingeborg Mohr, née Meyer 64

Figure 25 Jürgen in the garden of Tante Lotti and Onkel Franz 67
Figure 26 Jürgen at Tante Lotti's 68
Figure 27 Jürgen in uniform 70
Figure 28 Jürgen relaxing at a house in Russia. 73
Figure 29 Pflicht year at Dütschow, 1942 76
Figure 30 Charlotte and Manfred, summer 1944 86
Figure 31 Jürgen, June 1944 94
Figure 32 Charlotte and stepbrother Klaus 133
Figure 33 Michael in Royal Engineers uniform 134
Figure 34 Michael, studio portrait 137
Figure 35 Charlotte (right) and Frau Albert at the officers' mess 141
Figure 36 Charlotte, aged 20, with 'Madame de Pompadour' hairstyle 142
Figure 37 Charlotte by fountain, Wolfenbüttel, 1945 148
Figure 38 Onkel Herbert Dabelstein 152
Figure 39 Charlotte and Michael, Wedding Day, 1947 157
Figure 40 Michael's parents 158
Figure 41 Merryweather 167
Figure 42 Charlotte and Michael at Merryweather 168
Figure 43 Michael wearing his Légion d'honneur medal 184

Introduction

How Charlotte's Story Came to Be Related

This book records the recollections of Charlotte Fellows, née Krabbe, who was born in 1926, as recounted to the author during the years 2018–22. Whilst writing up my extended notes and research, I became aware that growing up in Nazi Germany had had an influence on Charlotte's philosophy for the rest of her life and would influence the choices she would make in a future society.

In *Charlotte's Story*, I have added dates of significant events to show that sometimes she was nearer to the theatre of war than she appears to have realized. It seems it was only at a very late stage in the war that she was abruptly forced into an awareness of the obviously wicked and inhuman treatment that was being enacted, which had previously gone unnoticed by her.

Charlotte grew up in Mecklenburg-Schwerin in the North of Germany, some distance from Hanover, Hamburg, and Berlin. She was part of an extended family, which would play a major role in her life at times of difficulty, including the death of her mother when she was aged 11 and then her father when she was aged 15. We shall see how she coped with all kinds of setbacks and obstacles and coped under pressure when positions of responsibility were put on her shoulders at a young age.

Because of Hitler

All these years after the ending of the war, Charlotte continues to feel very bitter at the loss of her brother, whom she describes as 'a lovely young man, who did not want to be in the war'. She said that he lost his life only because an ignorant, inadequate, insignificant man like Hitler, with his toothbrush moustache and odd hairstyle, was loved by millions and gained such power over a nation, of which a large proportion found him charismatic. He had the power to connect with people and to convince them that he could achieve what they wanted and needed. He connected with hidden prejudices and convinced the German people that they were racially superior to other nations and had been humiliated by decisions made at Versailles after WWI. He blamed the Jews for all that was wrong in society. Although there were those who did not feel that way, they and their voices were silenced. The German people as a whole needed and wanted to believe in his policies.

The Nazi Era

My first impression, gained from listening to Charlotte's stories of her life in Germany, was that her life appeared to have been largely separate from the influences of war. At first, it seemed to me that she had a series of experiences but to an extent seemed to live in her own series of bubbles, seemingly untouched by the Nazis, the war, and the bombing. Since researching the events, which she so clearly describes, I realize that, although she felt largely unaffected by Hitler or the ravages of war, her life was, in fact, being very much influenced by Hitler and the war. Unwittingly, she became a contributor to the war effort although she was largely isolated from knowledge of the horrors of the fighting and the evil of the death and concentration camps and widespread brutality and persecution suffered by millions and perpetrated by many. This was despite having a brother and a boyfriend caught up in the Wehrmacht. It appears too that she was unaware that she and other school children were being brainwashed. They had nothing with which to compare it. They had no experience of a life before Hitler and the Nazis, who were making their presence felt long before 1933, the year in which Hitler became Reich Chancellor. That was the year Hitler gained complete power over the German nation, enabling him to pursue his scheme to rid Germany of all the elements that he considered were undesirable. Charlotte was born in June 1926 and was a young child during these years. She was only seven years old when Hitler gained power. She thought children in all countries would sing songs about fighting for their countries.

They had experience of Adolf Hitler in complete power from 1934 until 1945, and before then had experienced the increasingly extreme behaviour of the Nazi Party, many children had not known a life without the Nazism. They had experienced years of teaching and propaganda in Nazi youth organizations and elsewhere. They were living in the years after the First World War when the German population was suffering from high unemployment, with the associated deprivation and lack of food of the economic depression. It seems that the German people were eager to embrace the solutions offered by Hitler and to point the finger of blame at certain sections of society as being the cause of the economic problems. When the Jews were singled out as scapegoats in Germany, as they were in other parts of Europe, anti-Semitism took hold.

Because of my ignorance, I was shocked when I learned that the best educated in Germany were amongst those in awe of Hitler and admired him; some even adored him and were capable of participating in a system that allowed them to commit atrocities in his name or force and enable others to do so. Among them were highly educated lawyers, psychologists, judges, and industrialists, who co-operated and enabled all the atrocities about which we know today, including the repulsive scientific experiments on living human beings. They were part of a system that treated millions of people as subhuman, singling out some categories as tainting Germany's image as a super race. An image of evil has been described by Hannah Arendt, one of the most important political thinkers of the twentieth century, as spreading like a fungus on the surface without roots. We see how people followed orders without thinking for themselves.

The Krabbe and Dabelstein Families

Charlotte Helene Krabbe grew up in Mecklenburg. It was a flat, agricultural area, part of which was bordered by the Baltic Sea and part of which was heathland. It also had rich meadows.

She was born on 20 June 1926 and had a brother, Jürgen Martin Friedrich Krabbe, who was born on 8 October 1923 but died on 10 July 1944, aged only 20. She lived with Andreas Wilhelm Friedrich Georg Krabbe, her father, who was born on 24 August 1885 and died on 29 March 1942, aged 56, when Charlotte was 15.

Her mother, whose name was Helene Elisabeth Martha Wilhelmine Dabelstein, nicknamed Muschi, was born on 19 Sept 1893 and died on 29 August 1937, aged only 43, when Charlotte was 11.

Charlotte later describes how she and her brother came to be parted by circumstances.

The Krabbes were a large family in Mecklenburg, some of whom were prominent. Many were teachers or in the Church.

Charlotte's great grandfather was Professor Otto Carsten Krabbe, a professor of theology and Rector of the University of Rostock 1840–73.[1] The Grand Duke of Mecklenburg-Schwerin handed Otto Krabbe a key and deeds at the memorial unveiling ceremony of the new university department, as he was responsible for building it. Otto's portrait hangs at the university to this day where his name is on the roll with his predecessors. But, more importantly and prominently, he is also depicted on a large bronze equestrian sculpture group in the palace square in Rostock. On a huge

---

[1] https://de.wikipedia.org/wiki/Otto_Krabbe

bronze statue, the Grand Duke is sitting astride a horse on a plinth. Around the sides of the plinth is a list of the good deeds of the Grand Duke and the name and portrait of Charlotte's great grandfather Otto being handed a key for the new university building by the Grand Duke. Charlotte came to realize later how important the Krabbe family were in Mecklenburg.

Figure 1 Theodor Martin Krabbe's grave

Charlotte's grandfather, Theodor Martin Krabbe, father of Andreas, was a Protestant clergyman, as was his twin brother, Charlotte's great uncle. Charlotte said it was impossible to tell them apart, especially when they were wearing their clerical garb. Andreas, her father, grew up with his father at Hohen Viecheln parsonage in Schwerin, together with his brother and his sister Grete, and his older half-sister Leni and her brothers Otto, Theodor, Carl, and Johannes, who were the children of Theodor's first wife. It seems that Andreas was not religious and probably attended church only on special occasions. His half-brother, Otto Krabbe, had a chicken farm at Kröpelin and was not ambitious.

After the war, during a holiday in Germany with her friend Edith, Charlotte saw a signpost pointing to her grandfather Theodor Martin Krabbe's parsonage at Hohen Viecheln, where she knew he was buried. A visit to the parsonage revealed that it was surprisingly tiny, with a thatched roof. The church had a separate bell tower. Only the clergy and their wives could be buried in the small churchyard and were not to be removed.

Charlotte's great uncle, Theodor's twin, was the resident pastor at a Protestant medical hospital in Ludwigslust, named Stift Bethlehem. Charlotte said that the nurses there wore special distinctive white caps.

Figure 2 Stift Bethlehem

Charlotte later learned of a clerical relative who was surnamed Krabbe and living in Ludwigslust, about whom she had not been told by her aunt (Tante Lotti) while she was living there. She now realizes that this was probably her great uncle's twin. She said that Tante Lotti kept herself apart from the Krabbe family, and Charlotte thinks she was perhaps envious of them. As her great uncle was at Stift Bethlehem in Ludwigslust, where Tante Lotti also lived, although she was on the opposite side of the long canal, Charlotte thinks it would be surprising if her aunt had not known of him because part of the institution where he was based is named Theodor Krabbe House. He was also pastor of the local church in Ludwigslust. She describes that as having a pink exterior. Charlotte has been told that her great uncle was the model for an oil painting of St Joseph in the church, which is still there today.

Charlotte has no knowledge of Nazi interference in the lives of either of the clerical twins, however, both Protestant and Catholic clergy elsewhere played a large role in opposing Hitler and the Nazis, for which they often paid a high price. She thinks it possible that the Nazis did not interfere here because it was a medical institution as well as a religious order.

Figure 3 Theodor Krabbe

Before the First World War, Charlotte's father Andreas, the youngest son of a clergyman, had moved abroad to work. He worked for an import and export company that produced sisal in Arusha, a German colony in Tanzania, East Africa. At the outbreak of the First World War in 1914, the British took over the German colony, and Andreas was interred by the British to prevent him from fighting on the German side. They sent him to India, although he was not part of the fighting force. Charlotte learned about his experiences as a prisoner because a partial diary, which he had written in an English exercise book, came into her hands later. He had written about the boiling heat in India and how the POWs were not given work to do. Andreas described how the British allowed the middle-class German prisoners a three-day break as there was no possibility of them escaping. Incongruously, they had to have Indian bearers carry their luggage to an area of lakes where they marched into the cool water, which was refreshing in the heat and a welcome taste of freedom.

Andreas wrote in his diary that he was grateful to the British NAAFI for giving the prisoners playing cards to help pass the time. He spent much of his time playing bridge. Although the war had ended in 1918, he was not allowed home to Germany until 1921 because any available transport was needed to repatriate the English. Charlotte said the diaries had to be written in English.

A photo survives, with Andreas's name written on the back of it in order to reserve it for him when he returned from his time in India. Charlotte is of the opinion that the Krabbe family were not attractive looking. One of them had inherited a physical defect that made his eyes look bulbous.

Figure 4 Andreas Krabbe

Charlotte's first family home was in Hamburg. Her parents, Andreas and Muschi Krabbe, were from a middle class family. In 1921, Andreas had returned from India to live in Hamburg, where Jürgen was born in 1923. It was the time of hyperinflation when the Papiermark was being devalued almost as soon as it was issued. People spent their money as soon as they received their wages in a race before its value dropped again. Charlotte and Jürgen's uncle, Muschi's brother Oscar Dabelstein, who lived in Hamburg, supported her family at this time and queued to get milk for baby Jürgen. This was in the time of shortages, which followed the First World War when there were queues for milk and adulterated bread.

Figure 5 The Krabbe family, Charlotte 2 months old, 24/8/1926

Too young to know an alternative way of life, Charlotte, who was born in June 1926 in a maternity home, would grow up in her formative years in a Germany that was in political turmoil, with extreme right-wing politics on the rise. The Storm Troopers (SA), in their khaki brown uniforms, were visible on the streets, committing extreme violence against the communists, whom Adolph Hitler and Ernst Röhm, an early member of the Nazi Party, both hated. These acts would be a prelude to the increasing violence that would follow.

Charlotte said that, when Hitler came to power, the Germans were hopeful that he would right the perceived wrongs imposed by the Treaty of Versailles, when the victorious nations had arranged imposed reparations, following Germany's defeat in the war. German lands were appropriated, and the economy was greatly depressed, with high unemployment and hyperinflation. Charlotte said her father Andreas was delighted when Adolf Hitler came to power to right the so-called wrongs. Andreas was, for a while, one of the unemployed until he became an employee of the American Vacuum Oil Company. He thought that, under Hitler, Germany would be prosperous again. Charlotte said the Germans wanted to be proud of who they were, and Hitler's preaching gave them hope that it would happen. Hitler began to construct new infrastructure, including autobahns right across Germany, to boost the economy, which began to take effect. This gave hope to the Germans, but presumably Andreas, among others, had yet to learn that part of Hitler's programme was to destroy all Jews. At first, Hitler hid the concentration camps, of which there would be so many, particularly in the East, including Poland, and it seems unwanted people simply disappeared into them and were murdered.

Figure 6 Krabbe Family with Tante Leni, c. 1926/1927

Tante Helene, known as Tante Leni, was Andreas's half-sister, who often spent time with them. She had a habit of visiting, to stay with the family. Nearly every weekend, the Krabbe family went out for a drive in their car, which seemed to Charlotte to be like a bus because it was square at the back. Charlotte had to sit in the back of the large car on the journey. But because she was too small to see out of the window, she would stand on the back seat, holding herself upright by holding onto a cord with a thick knot. She swung on this while looking out of the window.

Charlotte said that young German children, both boys and girls, wore Leibchen from when they could walk. These were composed of vests with buttons that had to be buttoned to a waistband of elastic (that could be bought by the metre) and stockings, but at times she refused to wear them.

The Move to Bielefeld

The family moved from Hamburg to Bielefeld, where Andreas was responsible for a large catchment area, possibly in a sales capacity, for which he needed a car. Here, Charlotte attended a nursery school.

Figure 7 Charlotte's sixth birthday at Bielefeld, 1932

Charlotte, the birthday girl', is at the front, with Jürgen at the rear of the six children, in front of a helper and a neighbour. Charlotte's sixth birthday party was held in the garden of their home at Bielefeld. She wore a garland of sweet peas in her hair, which had been created at a flower shop. Charlotte attended a kindergarten until the age of six, the age when all German children started school.

Figure 8 Jürgen and Charlotte, c. 1931

Hanover, 1932

By the time she started school, her family had moved to Hanover to live first at 71 and then 118 Hildesheimer Straße, in an area of flats for people in comfortable circumstances.

Figure 9 Hildesheimer Straße 118, Hanover

Charlotte described how blocks of ice, broken from the frozen lakes, were kept in a deep cellar and how the men who delivered them to the cities wore protection from the ice on their hands, a sort of glove with a strap, which was padded on the shoulder. They used to deliver ice blocks to their flat in Hanover on the fourth floor to Muschi, who was an invalid. It was stored in a ceramic container on four feet with drainage holes. Charlotte described how the containers were very heavy for the men climbing staircases.

Figure 10 Muschi Krabbe, sanatorium at Sülzhayn

At first, the family lived in a flat at no. 71. It had an upstairs balcony but no lift, so Charlotte's family moved into residence no. 118 on the lower floor because Muschi had difficulty breathing when climbing the stairs at no. 71. Muschi suffered poor health and was never well. She was in a sanatorium so often that the insurance ran out. Financial problems led at times to arguments between Muschi and Andreas. There were discussions on how to use Muschi's money from the sale of land at Rostock, which had been an inheritance.

Although she was unwell, Muschi took part in a programme called 'Winter Help' (Winterhilfswerk), whose aim was to help the poor. It seems there was acute distress in a large part of the German population, which needed help, but Charlotte felt that Muschi did not take enough care of herself. Charlotte remembers sugar crunching beneath her feet in the hall spilt from items Muschi had collected including flour and fat as well as sugar. She remembers food being sorted out on the hall table and being made up into parcels for distribution, which Muschi helped to distribute from their home.

While they were living at no. 71, the view from the balcony had been of an open area, in which there was a brick-built house, which was home to a family with six children, one of whom was in Charlotte's class at school. In the middle of the view, was Otto von Bismarck's Tower. It disappeared, as did the house, when the area was deliberately flooded as part of a job creation programme between March 1934 and 1936 when Charlotte was aged between eight and ten. The family, who were poor, would have had to leave their home. The Bismarck tower was dismantled in 1935 because it would be a danger to the leisure activities such as sailing on the huge artificial lake. The construction of the lake began in 1934 as part of Hitler's Nazi programme to revitalize the economy although it had been planned for some time before Hitler took over. The lake, which was constructed in a wide area of marsh, is named Maschsee where to this day water sports, pleasant meadow walks, and entertainments can be enjoyed. The work had created many jobs at a time of high unemployment. Muschi died about the time it was completed.

Figure 11 Christmas in Hanover

During the four weeks of advent, a wreath, made from a fir tree, was put in the centre of the dining table, with four candle holders. A candle was lit each week until Christmas arrived. 'Spekulatius' biscuits were made to special recipes.

Families celebrated St Nicholas's day on 6 December when children put one of their shoes out and wrote him a letter, requesting a gift. The shoe was left on the windowsill, and the next morning, the shoe would contain an orange, a tangerine, an apple, nuts, and sweets.

Figure 12 Christmas with Andreas Krabbe

Christmas was always celebrated, even in wartime. Once, when she lived in Hanover, they chose a Christmas tree from the market on 24 December. It was a special, quality one that was intended to last longer, and which they carried home. At home, it was put into an iron tree holder and decorated with items saved from past Christmases, including a silver trumpet. It was topped with an angel with wings or a silver star and decorated with real candles, which were lit. Charlotte said that there was no tradition of using holly or mistletoe. It was a small family occasion, and goose was eaten when they moved into the dining room at six o'clock on Christmas Eve, 24 December.

Charlotte would receive books for a present. She liked Sigrid Unset, a Norwegian author, and requested one each Christmas and for birthdays. Muschi liked Charlotte to wear a large white taffeta bow in her hair.

Figure 13 Charlotte, 4, Jürgen, 7 with Andreas and Muschi, Hanover, 1930

Charlotte said the running board of their square car provided a seat when they picnicked and had a blanket. It was quite a luxury at a time when not many families had cars.

Figure 14 Jürgen, 6, on his first day at school

All German children began school when they were six, so Charlotte's first day at elementary school (Berger Schule), was in Hanover in 1932, where she was living by then. There were no school uniforms, but for each child there was a fascinating custom, which was intended to make their first day at school less daunting. Each child was given a 'Zuckertüte', which Charlotte described as a cone made out of rolled-up cardboard and pointed at the bottom.[2] It was wrapped in pretty paper outside and in. It contained treats such as sweets and chocolates, with which it had been filled by their parents. Different parts of Germany had their own traditions and, it seems, still do to this day. Toys were added in some localities. Charlotte described being given a colourful wooden pencil box with a sliding top, containing items, including pencils, ink pens, a ruler, an eraser, and a special pencil for writing on a slate.

Charlotte said the school children had a daily bottle of milk and could choose to have warm or cold cocoa, or warm or cold milk. The little bottles were transported in metal trays. If the choice was for a warm drink, the bottles were warmed by standing them in hot water poured into a tray. A straw was provided to drink them.

The Third Reich, 1933

Hitler gained total power over the German nation, and a reign of unimaginable cruelty began.

Charlotte said there was a little girl in her class, who stood out as an outsider. On one occasion, the children had been told by their teacher that they were getting a new classmate. This was a time when Jewish children were barred from mainstream schools. Charlotte said the little girl appeared to be uneasy. She had a round face and looked so noticeably different. She did not fit in, and Charlotte wondered why she had come to that particular school. Charlotte

---

[2] https://en.wikipedia.org/wiki/Schult%C3%BCte

described the lonely child, who had black curly hair and a hooked nose. She felt she resembled some of the characters in the antisemitic propaganda material displayed on placards in the streets. No girls attempted to befriend the girl. They were prejudiced since they appeared to have nothing in common with her. Charlotte finds it hard to understand how the little girl was admitted to this school. It seemed a mystery. She felt sorry for the solitary girl, who looked so young, but she suddenly disappeared without any explanation as to why and where she had gone. Charlotte's memories are tinged with sadness and perhaps guilt, and it troubles her that she was not able to help the young girl.

Flowers for Hitler, 1934

There was one particular outing in the family car in 1934 in the month of June, when Charlotte was aged eight, which was rather different from their usual family outings. Her father drove Charlotte and her mother to the home of Herr Lutze, a friend of Muschi's, who was well known as a high-up official in the Nazi Party and a supporter of Hitler. He lived in a fashionable neighbourhood of Hanover. Charlotte remembers him as an educated man in an agreeable house, who seemed to be a gentleman. Herr Lutze had invited her mother to an event at his home, where Hitler was expected to arrive, and to whom Charlotte was to present flowers—a bunch of white asters, bought from a flower shop. But after much delay, while waiting for Hitler to arrive, Herr Lutze received information that Hitler would not be coming to the house and that instead they must go to a different part of Hanover, where Hitler, who was late, would be arriving by aeroplane.

The family immediately set off in a hurry to drive some distance to the venue at Am Schützenplatz, where they saw a marquee, which had been set up in an open area. It was a Schützenfest ('shooting festival') day, which was held each year in Hanover. In the mornings, at these events, there were shooting competitions when civilians belonging to a shooting club aimed at the bullseyes on targets. There was a funfair with roundabouts, merry-go-rounds with horses, music and lights, a marksman's booth with prizes, and stalls selling all kinds of items, including Lebkuchen ('gingerbread'), some in the form of hearts with messages written on them in icing. These might have 'I love you' or some such written on them. Ribbons or string were threaded through holes for them to be hung around the neck like a necklace. They can still be seen in Germany today.

Charlotte's father remained with his car while Muschi and Charlotte went into a marquee where they explained to Hitler's bodyguards that Charlotte was to present flowers to Hitler. Because Hitler liked to see children, they were allowed in and guided to sit at the front with many other children. It was a popular event. Charlotte and Muschi saw a line of black-booted storm troopers, standing legs astride with their backs to them. They allowed Muschi and Charlotte to stand and wait behind them although they did not have the necessary tickets. Charlotte was still holding the bunch of white daisies, in which a small paper Nazi flag on a stick had been inserted, she thinks by her mother. When Hitler arrived in the marquee, she had to squeeze between the black boots of the storm troopers to get to him to hand him the flowers. She remembers he passed them to someone else. Eight-year-old Charlotte was unimpressed by seeing Hitler after she had spent so much time idly waiting. Uncharacteristically, he did not speak while this was taking place. The drama for her was over in seconds. She did not appreciate the significance of the occasion and had just done what was expected of her. She found it a disappointing event after a tense time of waiting for something to happen. Usually, Hitler liked to give the appearance of loving children and wished to be filmed petting them, but not on this occasion.

Figure 15 Children greeting Hitler

Up to about this time, Muschi was an ardent supporter of Hitler and the SA (storm troopers), but shortly after this event, she became disgusted and left the party after hearing of the murder of Ernst Röhm in what Hitler called the 'Night of the Long knives' between 30 June and 2 July 1934. Röhm, an early member of the Nazi Party, had been a close comrade of Hitler, but Hitler found Röhm had become too powerful. Hitler arranged what was to happen to remove all opposition to him and to remove the power from the SA 'brownshirts', whose numbers, by January 1932, had reached 400,000 under Röhm. The assassinations were ordered by Hitler and organized by Himmler, who was then in sole power over the SS. The uniform of the SS under Heinrich Himmler's command was completely black, contrasting with the brown of the SA, led by Röhm, which made the appearance of the SS more menacing. It was not long after that event that Germany's President Hindenburg died, on 2 August 1934, and immediately Hitler was made Reich President in addition to his role as Reich Chancellor, with no curbs on his powers. Thus, he became dictator of Germany. He was then free to pursue the Holocaust unhindered, to achieve his aim of creating a free and pure German race.

Charlotte remembers that, after the night of the long knives in 1934, when she was aged eight, her mother, who had supported and trusted Ernst Röhm, was upset at his assassination and was disgusted at the killing by Hitler of his companions. Disillusioned, Muschi threw away her Nazi Party membership badge, which was a big metal badge. Up to this time, she had displayed the Nazi swastika flag, the Hakenkreuz, meaning 'hooked cross', outside their home. It is hard to comprehend today which of Röhm's qualities she admired. Charlotte thinks Röhm was not of the same ilk as the SS under Himmler and that his death was unfortunate, but today's historians have described someone who did not have peaceful ambitions and was anti-Semitic like Hitler. Because Muschi died in 1937, she did not have time to learn more about the rise and the power of the Nazi Party, nor did she have to answer for quitting Nazi Party membership. After Muschi died, Charlotte felt there was no enthusiasm in the family for the Nazi Party. Her mother had been a very enthusiastic supporter of Hitler until the killings in 1934. Hitler had such an enormous influence on people. Charlotte describes him as a confidence trickster.

A Wedding in Saxony, 1934

In 1934, when Charlotte was about nine years old, Muschi's cleaner at that time, who was from the countryside, asked if her daughter would like to come to a farmhouse wedding, and Muschi agreed that she could go. In Germany, at that time, it was the custom to have a dressmaker visit to make clothes and do repairs while spending a week living and eating with the family. Some seamstresses were very skilful. For the farmhouse wedding, the dressmaker made Charlotte a frock with stripes of pale blue, green, and yellow, with a large frill over the top. Charlotte's home was on a wide, busy road between Hanover and Hildesheim, separate from the other apartment blocks. She had to take a tram journey to get anywhere, otherwise it meant a long walk to and from the town. As a consequence, Charlotte had few school friends who visited her home, so she was looking forward to the wedding with excitement.

On the day of the wedding, her father took her to the farm in the village of Krähenwinkel and dropped her off, leaving her with some feelings of trepidation because she knew no one except the cleaner who had invited her. When she arrived at the farm in Lower Saxony, she saw a traditional, very wide thatched farmhouse with the typical, crossed horse heads carved from wood on the gable. On the roof was a storks' nest, which are common in Saxony, where storks arrived from South Africa each summer. She heard the clatter noise the storks made with their beaks. The front of the house had a central door for access to the living area, but the front of the farmhouse could be opened completely to reveal the ground floor. It was divided to accommodate farm machinery, and there was room for cattle that needed protection in winter and huge stables for the Arabian horses, which were trained in dressage skills. Lower Saxony today is still famed for the quality of its Arabian horses and the teaching of equestrian skills. The village remains unchanged.

Charlotte, who was wearing her new best dress, began to feel embarrassed very quickly. She soon realized she was overdressed when she saw that the other children were not wearing party clothes. But there was loads of food to eat, including the homemade Platenkuchen, a cake made of butter and almond pastry with yeast, oozing with butter, and topped with apples, plums, and crumble. She ate with relish in spite of feeling shy and quite out of place. But then there were two other occurrences that would lead to her further discomfort. She was puzzled when the other children seemed to find something about her was amusing until eventually she discovered that unbeknown to her they had pinned a pig's tail to the back of her frock. The tail was from the pig that had been slaughtered for the wedding feast. The children had done it to tease the 'townie' and make her feel she was an outsider. Then, to her great discomfort, she found that she had to sleep with the grandpa in his bed. The beds were built into the side of the walls and had little privacy because they were open to the stables. The grandfather was already asleep when she had to tuck herself in beside him. Luckily, she was so tired that she fell asleep immediately. Because of her overall discomfort, she does not remember details of the actual wedding beside those of the bride in her bridal clothes. This was a wedding party she thought she would never forget. We see that she has not forgotten it!

Figure 16 Muschi in the sanatorium, Sülzhayn

Death of Muschi, 1937

In 1937, Charlotte's mother, Helene Elisabeth (Muschi), died after time spent in a sanatorium and hospital. She died on 29 August 1937, aged only 42, when Charlotte was 10 and Jürgen not quite 14. She had been in poor health for some time and died in hospital of tuberculosis, which might perhaps have been contracted while she was visiting the poor people who lived in difficult circumstances. She had been in and out of a clinic in Berlin for three years and had undergone an operation to open her ribs to help her lungs, when TB was discovered. During this time, Andreas had to pay for her extended medical care. Charlotte remembers she felt hurt when she was not allowed to see her mother lying in her coffin. She had to stay in the car while Jürgen was allowed to do so. She said she always felt inferior to her brother. Though her aunts attended the funeral, they lived at too far a distance to be able to offer comfort to Jürgen and Charlotte, who were bored and lonely after their mother's death. Their father Andreas was often away and was not good with girls. There was no hugging.

Charlotte described her mother, Helene Elisabeth, who was born in 1893 as slim, elegant, and well dressed. She liked nice things. On one occasion, she took Charlotte to a chemist to buy a special Rosa Centifolia, which was a perfume in a pretty pink box. It had such a delicious smell that Charlotte could have wished to eat it. Her mother had two pairs of beautiful new shoes, which she had never worn. One pair was white and the other red. They had semi-high heels. After she died, Charlotte loved wearing them; they were the first shoes with heels that she had tried. Her feet were the same size as her mother's, and she said that she felt close to her mother when wearing them. Soon after her mother died, a school friend, whose father, Herr Heintz, was a wealthy factory owner, invited her to tea. She was collected from her home by a chauffeur and met at the door of the house by a butler in uniform, and there were maids who wore little white crescent shaped caps. Charlotte felt most uncomfortable. The family's home was too opulent for her liking. She had been invited because her mother had died, but she and the girl did not click as friends, and the visit did not lead to a closer relationship.

Figure 17 Jürgen, Charlotte, and Anneliese Hemmings at Tante Lotti's

Charlotte loved being with her mother's sister, Tante Lotti, at Otto-Kaysel-Straße 4 in Ludwigslust and spent all her school holidays with her and her uncle Franz. She spent more time with them when Muschi was in the sanatorium. She said that her brother Jürgen often preferred to stay at home with his friends and to ride the bike that he was given one Christmas. Charlotte greatly envied the bike. We can see, however, that he did visit Tante Lotti's. Charlotte has admitted she was jealous of her brother for a while. The bike in the picture belonged to Anneliese, Lotti's adopted daughter. It would play an important part in Charlotte's life.

When they were teenagers, Charlotte's brother Jürgen, who was 2½ years older than her, would bully her as other older brothers sometimes do. When they were ice-skating on frozen lakes in winter, he would push her over and encouraged other boys to do so, too. On one occasion at home, she was so cross with him she gave him an 'Ohrfeige', a box on the ear, then turned the key of one of the glass doors in the house so that he couldn't get at her. He was so shocked that he was polite to her after this.

The 1936 Olympics

The Summer Olympics Games, officially titled the Games of the XI Olympiad, were held in Berlin in August 1936. Charlotte was aged 11, so she was too young to be involved. To attend the games, you had to have a relative competing in the Games or be privileged in some way. Of course, the Games were a huge propaganda exercise for Hitler. Charlotte said she was never interested in sporting activities, but she was rather put out when an excited Jürgen, who was aged 12, was encouraged to attend the Games by a cousin, who was unknown to Charlotte then, and stayed with her for a week in Berlin. We can see that there was rivalry between Charlotte and Jürgen when they were young and Charlotte felt that Jürgen ruled her.

Hitler ordered any signs of anti-Semitism to be removed from sight of all the visitors to the Olympics. It seems that the world colluded in Hitler's attempts to prohibit Jewish athletes from competing in the games. But Hitler could not prevent Jessie Owens, a black athlete from the United States, from entering. He then won four gold medals and was the most successful athlete in Berlin. Hitler did not hide his displeasure because it undermined his attempt to promote German racial supremacy. More in line with his aims were the successes of the German athletes, who gained the most medals. Journalists reported to the world that they were impressed. There were many who took the games at face value and did not recognize that Jewish persecution was only hidden out of sight in order to dupe the world. The anti-Jewish propaganda posters that had covered large wooden walls had been removed and were out of sight. But, in reality, there were people who were already making attempts to evacuate Jewish children and families out of Germany to safety. They fully recognized the Nazi threat, and it seems that England, among others, had considered boycotting the Games.

The Communist Threat, 1936

In 1936, when she was about 10 years old, Charlotte's father took her on a sight-seeing visit to Hanover Linden, which was a very poor area of Hanover. She has no idea why her father did so, maybe it was because she had shown her curiosity. We can speculate that her father, like many others, saw the communists as a great threat. Charlotte said that Hitler liked flags and that they were everywhere. Even cars had flags on them, and she said, on that day, there was a sea of flags although it was a poor area and flags were expensive. On both sides of the street, flags were displayed everywhere from windows and from blocks of flats. The residents were displaying the red hammer and sickle flag of the communists and not the Nazi flag, which was red with a white sphere containing a large black swastika, one of which she herself had. When driving through the communist area that day, Andreas removed the flag that was displayed on his car although it was only for the motoring organization to which he belonged, but it had a small symbol in the middle that would have been seen as provocative by the people in the area through which they were driving. Charlotte said she felt they were among enemies. She said her father had been allowed to become a Nazi Party member because he had a car but was left to his own devices.

Kristallnacht, 1938

The most shocking and frightening occurrence for Charlotte happened when she was aged 12 and experienced what she describes as a horrible night in Hanover, which occurred between 9 and 10 November 1938. It became known as the infamous Night of Broken Glass (Kristallnacht). She remembers seeing broken windows and broken and splintered glass all over the pavements and was afraid. She saw that the shops owned by Jews had been ransacked and robbed and destroyed by the storm troopers and Nazi mobs. Included among the shops owned by Jews, was a lovely, good-quality china and glass shop, named Weitz, which she had enjoyed looking around. It was in the central shopping area where there were specialized quality shops. Charlotte's mother had a leather case that she called her shopping case, which she took with her to go and buy nice gifts from the shop. Its windows, along with those of all the other Jewish-owned shops, had been smashed, and their owners were gone. It is more than likely they had gone to concentration camps and were murdered, as happened to others in other places throughout Germany. Some Jews had feared what might be coming and had emigrated to America and England. Some had migrated to France, but they soon learned to their cost that it would not provide a safe haven for long. From France, thousands were sent to concentration and death camps when neighbours informed on neighbours. In reality, Jews were probably not safe in any country.

Charlotte learned only later that, during Kristallnacht, Hanover's synagogue and others throughout Germany had been burnt down and that the businesses and homes of Jews were destroyed or painted with anti-Jewish slogans. These had belonged to innocent, defenceless people. It seems that the attacks were committed partly by Nazi mobs, including members of the SA (Sturmabteilung) or Brownshirts (Storm Troopers), and some by citizens who watched with excitement then joined in. But there were other citizens who were horrified at the treatment of the Jews. The broken and shattered glass presented a deeply shocking scene for a 12-year-old schoolchild, whose mother had died and who had no one to talk to and comfort her. Her father seemed distant because his mind was on his work and he was often away. One night, when she was sleepless and lonely and needed comforting, Charlotte snuggled into her father's bed, but he turned his back on her, so she crept back to her own bed, feeling rejected. She does not know what he thought about the destructive behaviour they had witnessed.

Propaganda

Some of the Nazi anti-Semitic propaganda to which Charlotte was exposed took the form of a double-page spread, displayed on a wooden display stand with glass doors, in front of which mostly men used to congregate and read. Alongside them, she said, there were also communist and socialist newspapers and more worthy local papers to give some semblance of normality, but these were not eye-catching. Besides being sold at newsstands, *Der Stürmer*, a virulently anti-Semitic newspaper created by Julius Streicher, was put on display in the specially constructed display cases all around Germany. Theyg were everywhere and full of hate, calling for the extermination of the Jews. They could not be missed because there were so many at strategic places such as railway stations. Some of it was so unpleasant, it was abhorrent to many Germans, but its purpose was to incite hatred of the Jews, and Hitler supported it.

Charlotte described examples of the anti-Semitic propaganda. She described how there were placards and lots of caricatures of Jewish people, which were so horrific that she could not bear to look at them and does not like even to recall the images today because they were so unpleasant. Some examples showed people dressed all in black, with distorted faces and exaggerated hooked noses. They were made to appear malignant and frightening. When she was aged 12, she tried to read the posters but found them too awful. She said the propaganda was effective because she said she perceived it to be the truth, and it made her afraid of the Jews even though she knew Jews who were perfectly ordinary and did not resemble the caricatures. They were described in derogatory terms. Charlotte's feelings of fear of the Jewish people were reinforced when Jewish adults and children were ordered to wear a yellow star to set them apart so that they were easily identifiable.

The anti-Jewish newspapers, including Julius Streicher's *Der Stürmer*, and their propaganda continued until February 1945, close to the end of the war, but by then, there were very few Jews left in the towns. It was an effective tool, which helped Hitler and the Nazis sway the German public's opinion against the Jews. Julius Streicher's anti-Semitic paper, which was produced even before the Third Reich began, made him a multi-millionaire, but he was not able to enjoy that wealth in the long term. In 1946, he was tried at

Nuremburg, alongside other notorious Nazis. Still virulently anti-Semitic, he was among those convicted of crimes against humanity and executed.

Charlotte said that Hitler's henchmen, in their separate ministries, were prominent in her daily life. They were visible in newspapers and recorded on radio programmes. Göring issued new laws. Joseph Goebbels, in his Ministry of Public Enlightenment and Propaganda, was brilliantly in charge of propaganda and censorship. He ensured that anti-Jewish propaganda in all its forms was everywhere in everyday life and aimed at the youngest to the oldest members of society. Although they were successful and clever, or because they were successful and clever, day after day Jews were portrayed as robbing people of money and as liars. It could not be escaped. It was insidious. Every day radio officials had to take care what they said. They had to appear to be neutral.

Heinrich Himmler and the Black Shirts, the SS (Schutzstaffel) under his command, were feared and hated. Their numbers increased to at least a million. Himmler's mission was to rid the world of the Jewish race, and he worked to that end up to the very last opportunity by ordering the rounding up of victims to be exterminated. He was the main architect of the Holocaust. Himmler set out on his quest to rid the nation of 'undesirables'. He created concentration camps and death camps and was responsible for the death of millions of Polish and Soviet citizens. Hitler appointed Himmler to more and more powerful positions because Hitler thought his tactic of fear was going to ensure the success of Nazi Germany. And he used his power to press on with the doctrine of hate.

Charlotte thinks the German elite was more concerned about the dangers of communism than of Nazism, and they blamed the Jews for that. The Jews were victims of many conspiracy theories, which were created to give a reason to punish them and have them taken to the concentration and death camps. History tells us there has always been anti-Jewish feeling in many countries and not only in Germany, even before Hitler exploited it to set in motion the Holocaust when thousands of innocent people in Germany and occupied countries were being rounded up and disappeared. Charlotte said she was herself unaware of it except perhaps on one occasion at school.

Had Charlotte's mother Muschi not died in 1937, it is likely she would have been sent for re-education at the very least for daring to leave the Party. Pastors and others were reported to the authorities. There were spies everywhere. The Gestapo arrested people, and torture was used. They had the powers to put people into a concentration camp to be re-educated. During the war, the numbers detained increased, and it seems people disappeared in their thousands without anyone really remarking on it. They were never to be seen again.

Re-Education, 1938

Even before the start of the war, there were already German camps for re-education into Nazism. Teachers had to spend time at the camps. Charlotte's cousin Sunihild, a primary school teacher, was scathing and said wryly that she had been re-educated. Pastors, as we have learned, attended such camps. The camps, which had begun before the war, were used for political education of all kinds of people who questioned Nazi ideas. Her cousin apparently said that what she learned went in one ear and out the other, but people did not talk about what they learned there. Teachers were told what they could teach. Later, the camps could be used as forced labour camps.

As we have already learned, Charlotte's paternal grandfather was a Protestant pastor in Ludwigslust, while his twin brother, her great uncle, was also a pastor and the pastor at a Protestant hospital. At first, pastors could be sent to detention centres but allowed out again after undergoing re-education, as were teachers. Charlotte said this created a false illusion because Hitler's motive, when he created the concentration camps, was to use them to get rid of the Jews and other groups, including gypsies, homosexuals, the mentally ill, and absolutely anyone who did not conform to the Nazi ideal of a super race. These certainly were not allowed out of the camps.

Charlotte considers that Hamburg was sympathetic to the Nazis but that Hanover was not, but future events would show that it was not that simple. Charlotte said her aunts were not sympathetic to the Nazi cause. Tante Lotti was deaf, and she spoke rather loudly, which could have caused a problem if she had expressed her views out loud. Because of this, Charlotte did not like going into the town with her because she spoke loudly and made personal remarks about people, which could be overheard. Any anti-Nazi remarks that were overheard could have got her into trouble. Charlotte said the middle classes, including teachers, would not be sympathetic to the Nazis. There was a lot of feeling against Hitler, but people who spoke out against him were arrested. Perhaps there was acquiescence, with some wanting a quiet life, so they buried their heads in the sand.

Charlotte told me that she was not aware of fearing the authorities. But then again, she said people got on with the tasks they were allotted and probably without questioning the orders. She also mentioned the fear of God in Germany to do as one was told. No one was checking, but people followed the laws anyway. She said a feeling of being besieged unites a country.

Figure 18 Charlotte, aged 12 (top row, third from left), school group photo, 1938, class 3a with classmates, including Edith and Merigart

Figure 19 School assembly hall

Post-war historians have described some of the ways Hitler and the Nazis controlled what children were taught at school.

Because of Hitler schoolbooks were re-written to give his interpretation of German history and Germany's place in the world.

And to make sure that this was taught teachers were educated at the special camps before returning to the classroom. Saying Heil Hitler was a normal part of each day for every schoolteacher and child. Charlotte said that at all schools the children had to say Heil Hitler throughout the day,k at the beginning of each lesson and change of teacher. Charlotte said she and her young friends at the elementary school including her friends Edith and Merigart all did it in a rather flippant way except for the first lesson of the day when the teacher stood on the dais. In assembly they had to do it formally with arm stretched out high for one minute. She felt it was simply a gesture without meaning. But of course its intention was very much to keep Hitler firmly in the daily picture and was part of their indoctrination. They had to sing Nationalistic songs. In assembly when children were noisy saying Heil Hitler, immediately quietened them. Her friend Edith's chosen subjects were languages and science while Charlotte was more interested in the Arts and languages. They sat next to each other and Charlotte would write Edith's essays for her and Edith would do Charlotte's maths for her.

Hitler's views infiltrated all parts of life and society. Charlotte had thought that Hitler had ordered German handwriting, known as Sütterlin script, to be taught in schools, but in fact, in September of 1941, Hitler banned the continuation of the teaching of the Sütterlin script in Volksschulen (elementary schools) because officials realized that most of the occupied European countries under their control could not read Sütterlin. Charlotte had been taught it in her elementary school when she began in 1932 when it was still the official script. She said it was a big change to experience when she went to the grammar school where she had to write using Latinized Script. But evidently though Sütterlin handwriting was no longer being taught in Germany's schools after 1941, it continued to be used during the War. Older Generations that had already been taught the Sütterlin style knew no other way of writing. Sütterlin script is found in Soldbücher 'pay books' and letters, written throughout the war.

For part of their education children were taught that Germany was badly treated by the Versailles Treaty and was burdened by the heavy war reparations. They learned that Hitler was popular because he had refused to pay the war reparations. The pupils were taught patriotic songs about fighting for the fatherland. Charlotte thought this was what was normal in schools and that it would be the same in other countries and not just in Germany. They were taught that they were in the middle of Europe surrounded by hostile countries that were threatening them. In fact, the unexpected and severe Wall Street stock market crash in America in October 1929 was partly the cause of a worldwide depression, by which Germany was very much affected. Hitler exploited the situation as a reason to aid him to gain power. A whole generation was indoctrinated by Nazi teaching while at school and during their leisure pursuits. School textbooks were rewritten to include the Nazi teaching.

Charlotte said the school children had to make a financial contribution to Namibia because it was still a German colony. It seems that fairly recently there have been moves by Germany to negotiate compensation for past treatment of the natives.

Hitler Youth, etc.

At the age of 10, in 1933, Charlotte's brother Jürgen joined the Deutsches Jungvolk movement, which all boys aged 10–14 had to join. Its main purpose was to indoctrinate them in Nazi ideology. All other traditional youth groups, such as the Boy Scouts, were banned. Other groups were either disbanded or absorbed into the movement, which provided opportunities such as summer camps and sports facilities that were open only to members. In March 1939, it became mandatory for all Germans aged 10 to 18 to join the Nazi youth movement. The Hitler Youth was for boys aged 14–18. The parents of boys who failed to join were threatened with criminal prosecution. Besides the mixture of scouting activities, including camping, the minds of the youth, including Jürgen's, were subjected to Nazi propaganda. The movement focused on Hitler and created young Nazis trained to be proud and ready to fight for Germany. It seems some did attempt to resist the teaching and wished to spread the word against Hitler, including some students at university named the White Rose group, who were opposed to Nazi ideology, but the Gestapo treated them ruthlessly. Their names are among the names remembered as resistance heroes today.

For the girls, there was a separate section of the Nazi youth movement, the Jungmädelbund 'Young Girls' League' for girls aged between 10 and 14 years. The Bund Deutscher Mädel (BDM) 'League of German Girls' was the organization for those aged 14–18 years. Charlotte said she, like everyone else, went into the Jungmädelbund when she was aged 10; otherwise she would have been the odd one out. She said everyone was expected to be in it, and everyone was keen. A whole generation was, unbeknown to themselves, undergoing indoctrination by the Nazis. Charlotte thought it fun when she was little. On Saturday afternoons, they used to gather, and their shoes and socks were inspected.

She had to a wear a special uniform of a navy skirt, and a white blouse with a scarf tucked into a woggle, and white ankle socks, but she chose knee length socks, and brown shoes. White socks stood out when they were parading in lines. An emblem had to be sewn on. At times, she would not conform and would not wear the stipulated dark brown stockings in winter because she hated the elastic suspenders that held them up. She did not always follow the rules but said no one bothered. She said she often had frostbitten or blue knees. The purpose of the League was to train girls to be good at domestic tasks, to prepare them to be good housewives and mothers. They were encouraged to aim to marry and have several children and would be paid more money for each extra child. A medal would be awarded if they had five children. While in Hanover's Nazi youth movement, Edith, her school friend from a young age, was a leader in a higher rank. They had to stay in their correct rank, but they remained friends into the future, as we shall see.

Herbert Albrecht at one time was the Gauleiter or district Nazi leader for the Mecklenburg area. Gauleiters were hated and were more likely to enforce rules. Charlotte said a climate of fear was created, and she always felt she was being watched, though she didn't know why. The children would tease each other by calling them Gauleiter as a sort of term of abuse. At school, naughty children were made to stand in a corner with their backs to everyone and be silent. Anyone misbehaving would be threatened with the possibility of being sent to somewhere that was not very nice. People were used to seeing wire fences but could not imagine what was going on behind the fences.

One summer, Charlotte went on a duty training camp to train to be a leader apprentice on a week's camp at Balfron on a Frisian Isle in the North Sea. There, the girls had to sleep in a bell tent, lying in a ring with their feet towards the tent pole. They lay on straw-filled paillasses, which got flatter and flatter as the days went by, and the floor harder and harder. Charlotte said at least the straw smelled nice. There were no washing facilities, and because she so hated the latrines, where they had to sit on a beam over a ditch, Charlotte was completely put off. And she could not manage to go to the loo for the whole of the week there. She hated the whole experience; it was not for her.

War, 1939

Hitler took a step too far, when, in September 1939, after already having invaded Czechoslovakia, he ordered the march into Poland between 1 and 6 September 1939. France and Britain then declared war on Germany on 3 September 1939. Charlotte heard the declaration of war announced on the radio. She was 13 years old, and Jürgen was aged 16.

Charlotte was living with her father and brother in Hanover when it was bombed very early on. After Germany had entered Poland and war on Germany was declared, the RAF dropped propaganda leaflets from their planes on 4 September 1939 but very soon were dropping bombs. In 1940, during the month of May, Hanover was bombed several times by the allies, but there would be far more to follow.

Charlotte remembers one occasion in 1940 when she was playing in Hanover with other children at the home of a friend of her mother's and her daughter Merigart, a friend of Charlotte's, that they had all rushed up to the balcony where, with the family, they watched as an oil refinery was under attack from English bombers. During some raids, cement factories and oil tanks were targeted. Some were hit, and the tracers burned like fireworks of green and red. Charlotte described amazing colours caught in the searchlights. She said she wasn't afraid that day as she thought it was only temporary because the war was expected to be over very quickly. People would learn that that was not to be.

Her friend's father was a librarian to the King of Hanover. The mother, who had been a great friend of Charlotte's mother, lived in a ménage à trois. Her husband had lung problems and could hardly breath. A young Charlotte had not realized the significance of the arrangement. The home harboured a lodger, who was younger than Merigart's mother, and Charlotte thinks he was hiding from Hitler because he was a pacifist and did not want to be conscripted.

At her home in the Hildesheimer Straße, on a main road in Hanover, Charlotte could smell the smoke during raids. It seemed to her to be both frightening and exciting, but she said as a teenager she wasn't afraid. Later, when her family heard the air raid sirens they went down into the cold cellar. They were ordered to do so, and later there were wardens to enforce that rule. The newspapers reported the raids but not the damage that had been inflicted by them.

As we have seen, at the start of the Second World War in 1939, Charlotte was aged 13, and her father by then was a widower because her mother had died in 1937 when Charlotte was only 11 years old. Charlotte was living with her father and brother Jürgen with a succession of housekeepers, who were not good; some were dishonest and stole linen until the arrival of one named Erna Benske. She had worked for Muschi and loved cleaning and appeared to be reliable but was in Charlotte's eye a most unpleasant person, whom she hated. She didn't look after or mother Charlotte and Jürgen, who were bored and lonely. The flat had only three bedrooms, of which Andreas had one and Jürgen another. Surprisingly, and not very pleasantly for Charlotte, she had to share her own room with Erna. Before she died, Muschi had made Charlotte's room special for her by having it decorated in pink. The washstand and a chest of drawers were also pink. She had her room to herself during a gap of a few months when Erna left the house before she returned with a new baby boy named Klaus, who was at the crawling stage. Charlotte felt a sense of resentment when Erna and the baby were expected to sleep in her room with her. She felt her home was not her own. It seems that Klaus was not Andreas's son and was not adopted by him, but nevertheless Andreas was glad to have Erna back to look after the household. Charlotte said it was because men are helpless. She gave one example, describing how Andreas had turned to the man who delivered the coke for the central heating, to ask how it should be turned on because he had no idea how to deal with it.

Meanwhile, Charlotte had looked inside Erna's chest of drawers in their shared bedroom. There she discovered letters, which should not have been in there, that had been written by her mother and someone that Charlotte knew nothing about, who had a daughter named 'Asta', who had had an abortion. She did not stay looking at the letters for long because she felt guilty for prying, but the discovery of the hidden letters made Charlotte realize that Erna was not a nice person. Then, one day when Charlotte was 13, in 1939, and was being argumentative, Erna, who was washing a floor, threw the dirty wet floor cloth in her face. This was too much. Charlotte decided she could not live in the same house as Erna any longer and ran away.

She ran to the home of Merigart, whose mother, Frau Meyer, had been the close friend of Muschi. It was the same house where she had watched the bombing taking place.

Charlotte explained that Merigart's mother chose the name Merigart because she believed in old Germanic names, and at the time there was a move away from biblical names. The Meyer family lived in a select block of flats in Hanover. Charlotte's father Andreas went to fetch her home, but she refused to go with him. She could not bear to live with the housekeeper and told her father about the letters. When Andreas took her home to collect her clothes, Erna was angry with her for telling Andreas about the letters and started to attack Charlotte until Andreas intervened.

Charlotte had two aunts, and her father arranged that she could live in Ludwigslust with her mother's sister, Charlotte Hemmings, known as Tante Lotti, who was her godmother and the aunt she liked most, with whom she had spent all her school holidays and a year when Muschi was ill in a sanatorium. Charlotte had attended a primary school in Ludwigslust during those times. As it happened, before Charlotte had left her mother's friend's flat to live with Tante Lotti, she contracted tonsillitis so remained with the Meyers for two or three weeks until she had recovered. Merigart's mother, who was kind, nursed her. To treat a high temperature at that time, the solution was to wrap her in a cold sheet and a waterproof sheet and then a woollen blanket to cause her to perspire and bring down her temperature. Nevertheless, she recovered.

The schools broke up for the summer in July for a six-week break before returning for the new school year in the first week of September, but for Charlotte this would be her last year at a Hanover school.

Although it was not known by anyone who did not have a crystal ball and least of all by Hitler and his henchmen, it was about this time that Hitler would reach the height of his powers, but unbeknown to him, he was already on a downward path to his and Germany's self-destruction.

Figure 20 Charlotte, 14, class 5a, at school in Hanover, 1940

Figure 21 School group photo, class 5a, Hanover, 1940

It was time for Charlotte to attend a secondary school and leave her school friends Merigart and Edith in Hanover because she was moving to live in Ludwigslust. But both girls would re-enter Charlotte's life, and in a strange encounter Charlotte would one day play a vital part in Edith's life when she gave her some important advice that may well have saved her life. Edith would stay longer at the Hanover school to prepare for a university place.

As soon as she had recovered from the bout of tonsillitis at Merigart's home, Charlotte moved to Tante Lotti's in Ludwigslust and away from Hanover. At her new school in Ludwigslust, she made what would prove to be another lifelong close friend.

Life with Tante Lotti and Onkel Franz

Tante Lotti was Charlotte's godmother. She lived in a big house at Ludwigslust, a town that was known for its rich heritage. The house stood alone when it was built but later others were built nearby. She was a headmaster's wife, and while living with her, Charlotte attended the boys' grammar school at Ludwigslust where her Onkel Franz Hemmings was the headmaster. In the mixed class, she was one of only five or six girls attending. There were no Lyceums for girls nearby, as the nearest was at Schwerin. Charlotte said she hadn't a clue what was going on while at her uncle's school. She had a new form of Latin script to learn and a change from learning French as a second language to learning English as a second language. She mentioned a lesson on Ovid and Greek wars in Latin, about which she knew nothing. Unlike girls' schools, which had a different curriculum, at the boys' schools, the pupils were taught about battles. After school in the evenings, Tante Lotti insisted on instructing Charlotte in French.

Tante Lotti could not have children but had adopted Anneliese, who became the source of a lot of worry. Although unmarried, Anneliese bore three baby boys in a Berlin clinic, from where they were to be put in an orphanage or adopted because of the shame felt about babies born out of wedlock. It seems Anneliese expressed no motherly feelings at that time. Tante Lotti became unhappy about the orphaned babies and allowed Anneliese to bring the third baby, named Robert, home. He had been about to enter an orphanage. She couldn't bear to send him away. Robert called Tante Lotti 'Oma', the German name for 'grandma'. Although Charlotte had not known the reason for it whilst living at her aunt and uncle's, when Anneliese had spent some time away, it was to give birth to one of the babies. Robert, as we shall see, grew up to be a very caring person.

One night, while living with Tante Lotti, Charlotte had to give up her bedroom and sleep with her cousin Anneliese to make room for a visitor. She discovered to her surprise that she had a maternal grandmother. Her mother and father had hidden that information from her. She learned that her grandmother Helene Dabelstein, Muschi's mother, had left her husband and five children, including Muschi, who was aged only five. She remarried, becoming Helene Heyne, lived in Hamburg and had another daughter, named Asta. Asta was the supposed cousin that Jürgen visited to view the Olympics in 1936. Asta was actually a half-sister of Muschi and an aunt of Charlotte and Jürgen. Unlike her sister Lotti and her three brothers, Muschi did not forgive her mother for leaving her and did not speak to her again. Charlotte said her Grandma Helene was tall, elegant, and smart, with white hair, but she did not experience a family feeling towards her, although Tante Lotti was welcoming to her mother. When her grandmother Helene died, she left in her will to Charlotte a silver soup ladle, which, for some unknown reason, Tante Lotti and Onkel Franz did not pass on to her. Charlotte says she was cross and felt deprived, but nevertheless it did not change her perception of her aunt being lovely.

Tante Lotti could be critical of the Krabbe side of the family. Charlotte thinks it was possibly because the Dabelstein side of the family enjoyed intellectual pursuits. But the Krabbe family was itself successful and had prominence in Mecklenburg, so Charlotte could see no reason for her aunt's antipathy. She feels it might have been jealousy. One day, Tante Lotti would be given the opportunity to change her opinion about one member of the Krabbe family.

Tante Lotti had an overworked maid, who served tea in a black frock and white apron. Tante Lotti used to summon her to the table by ringing a bell. Charlotte said the maid's life was lonely. She had to eat on her own in the kitchen and be at the family's beck and call. But at the outbreak of war, employees such as maids had to leave their employers to do war work. Some of the work they were ordered to do was work on munitions. Charlotte thinks that the maid would have been pleased have the opportunity to leave her aunt to do war work. I am not sure that some of the work would have been considered to be an improvement.

An occasional lighter side to living with Tante Lotti and Onkel Franz Hennings was experienced when Jürgen spent his two weeks annual leave with them and he was allowed to have a party. The adults would retreat into another room, and Tante Lotti would remove her hearing aid so she wasn't disturbed by the party noise. The effects of a home-concocted liqueur evidently enlivened the mood of the party. Charlotte described how pure alcohol was bought from a chemist, procured after a little flirting with him. Very strong coffee was added to it that was probably brewed from coffee beans they still had in the house. Charlotte said it was very nice but probably lethal. This may have been at the time when Jürgen finished at the officer training camp at Bamberg. Jürgen was conscripted in 1941.

Charlotte used to play with other children on the building site close to her aunt's home, amongst half-built new houses, which would become the homes of her aunt's future neighbours. There was an unprotected lime pit, which the children avoided and of which Charlotte was scared. The builders regularly chased the children away from the site, but Charlotte said there was plenty of time for them to play when the builders went home. She said the site was like a magnet. The children used to build tunnels in the sandy soil, which were very unsafe. She said it was fun and she would lose all sense of time and forget to go home until Tante Lotti, tired of shouting her name, beat a large gong to summon her. Charlotte said it was so embarrassing. Tante Lotti, because she was deaf, had no idea that Charlotte had been putting herself in danger.

Figure 22 Onkel Franz

Memories of Onkel Franz

Tante Lotti's house in the small town of Ludwigslust was very large, with a large cellar and a garden that her uncle Franz loved. Charlotte enjoyed helping him to plant dahlias.

She remembers a big oak tree in her uncle's garden. She also remembers the feelings of pleasure she had when her quiet uncle took her mushrooming, although she remembers that she found balancing on the front of his bike very uncomfortable. Onkel Franz was a biologist and very knowledgeable about mushrooms, so they were able to gather them without the risk of poisoning themselves. Charlotte explained that the mushrooms were cooked slowly with onions in butter. Her uncle explained the names of trees and leaves in the woods, which Charlotte so enjoyed learning about because biology was her favourite subject. She remembers his quiet study, lined with books.

Figure 23 Ludwigslust postcard

Ludwigslust, which means 'Ludwig's pleasure', was a former ducal residence, 40 km south of Schwerin. Charlotte describes it as small and charming, with wide cobbled streets. It is known for its rich heritage, especially the famed Ludwigslust Palace known as the Versailles of the north, which was one of the residences of the grand-ducal family of

Mecklenburg-Strelitz. Charlotte described Ludwigslust as a gem of a town inside a town wall with a gate. She preferred living there rather than in the city of Hanover, which was her home. It had a wide avenue of linden trees approaching the grand duke's residence, with houses for the servants and an artificial canal. Charlotte said that, even to a child's eye, it was attractive. Its houses were close to each other, possibly terraced. Charlotte said it was a bit like an iced cake with turrets that seemed to exist in a different timeline and that even today the town centre with its town gate has not changed.

Tante Lotti always kept chickens, for which she would beg potato peelings from neighbours to feed them. When she was short of food for the chickens, she sent Charlotte to take corn or barley she had acquired to the corn mill to be ground. The meal was mixed with the potato peelings and water, put in a pot, and cooked on the gas stove. It was then fed to the chickens. Whilst it was cooking, the mixture had a very distinctive smell, which pervaded the kitchen. But without this feed, there would have been no eggs. This was before the era of mass-produced chickens and eggs.

Another of Charlotte's tasks, whenever living at her Tante Lotti's, was one that she hated. When her aunt heard from a nearby smallholding that a cow had been milked, she sent Charlotte to collect milk in a metal can that had no lid. Charlotte had to cycle on her cousin Anneliese's bike, which was too large for her, to the smallholding where the cow's warm milk was ladled into the can. Because she couldn't reach the saddle, she had a most uncomfortable journey, wobbling and bumping on the cobbled streets. On the way home, the sloshing milk threatened to spill out of the can because of the shaking it received on the cobbled streets in the heart of picturesque Ludwigslust. At times,

Charlotte had to resort to getting off the bike and walking. The whole experience was made even less pleasant because Charlotte couldn't bear the sickly aroma of the milk.

In 1940, with her move to Ludwigslust, there were not enough girl officers for a League of Girls Guild, so after a selection process by the girls by size, she became a group leader in the under-fifteens' section. She told me that she had set up the group herself by getting six girls together who were at the Boys' school, including Barbara. They were now of an age to be in the Bund Deutscher Mädel (BDM), which was for girls aged between 14 and 18 years. She said she was able to choose what she wanted the girls to do. There were cloth badges to work for in this youth guild. Charlotte described it as a wild and independent group, not conforming to any rules. Because she was not interested in housekeeping badges, she concentrated on organizing the outdoor interests and activities of games and picnics, which she enjoyed. Charlotte is amused today when she recalls how she set the standard and inspected the girls' appearance and by the fact that they did what she told them to do. She said they pretended to be a Nazi group, but did not conform. They made up their own rules and did not wear the correct-length socks. They would say Heil Hitler but Charlotte said she never admired Hitler. Somehow, they managed to escape attention. She said Tante Lotti seemed to find it amusing and laughed when Charlotte went off to her activities. Perhaps we can understand why.

While living with Tante Lotti, when aged 14, Charlotte used to visit Barbara at her home in Ludwigslust. She was one of the few girls attending her uncle's school in Ludwigslust at the same time as herself. At Barbara's home, she was intrigued by the sight of her friend's father, Herr Lorenz, who had been badly injured when he was a pilot in

WW1. He had lost one of his legs and an eye, and the side of his face was damaged. But she said he did not let his injuries hinder him. He had an artificial wooden leg and separate foot, which she saw him take off when she stayed overnight—no doubt primitive prosthetics, compared with what would be available today. He also had a glass eye, which she saw him remove. He always had a group of Luftwaffe ex officers/pilots around him, who seemed to be connected to the aerodrome that was across the road. Its Mess was near to the flat. Charlotte and Barbara felt important when making drinks for the men and doing the washing up. There was a smoky atmosphere in the house. Charlotte said it felt glamorous because it was the world of grownups. It may also have been that there was an air of mystery about it. Charlotte thinks the men were not Nazis and were very anti-Hitler and perhaps may possibly have been involved in sabotage, but she is not sure of that. On the quiet, they made jokes about Hitler and the Nazis, whom they judged to be beneath them. Charlotte spent a lot of time with the family. On one occasion, all the family were invited to a neighbour's wedding, and Charlotte stayed at it because of the nice food, although she had not told Tante Lotti that she was going to be late. Charlotte expected her aunt would be cross with her when she got home, so she persuaded Barbara to bicycle home with her. Charlotte was surprised when unexpectedly Tante Lotti did not tell her off, especially when her aunt said, 'even though Barbara is with you, you need not have worried about what I would say'.

This would not be the only time Charlotte would use Barbara to boost her morale, and the pair of them on more than one occasion would find themselves companions in very unexpected, even testing, circumstances.

Charlotte finds it difficult to define what she considered was a Nazi, although she felt that they were identifiable. They visibly showed enthusiasm, displayed flags and perhaps attended rallies. Charlotte said the Germans had a liking for flags. On the first of May, flags were always flown in celebration. No doubt, Nazis showed their enthusiasm for the party, while others not of that persuasion would have kept quiet. Medals were given to those who paid a fee to became a National Socialist.

Charlotte described how every town hall had a cellar (Ratskeller), where people could socialize and have refreshments. Her uncle Franz attended a Ratskeller weekly. Here in the evenings men played Skat, a card game similar to bridge. It was harmless, and members were not Nazis. The Ludwigslust flag was on display in there.

Then, in 1940/41, when Charlotte was aged about 14/15, her circumstances underwent yet another change, and the familiar routine she had settled into came to an abrupt end. Tante Lotti told Charlotte she must go back home to live with her father because he had remarried and she now had a new mummy. Unfortunately, her father had married the hated Erna, his former housekeeper, on 6 September 1941. Erna became Charlotte's stepmother. This was very unwelcome news for Charlotte, who certainly did not want to go home to live, and once more the housekeeper, now Frau Krabbe, was the reason. Charlotte felt cross and upset and a sense of rejection at her aunt's decision and to this day wonders why her lovely aunt asked her to leave.

For various reasons, some relatives were unable to offer Charlotte a home, so, in desperation and as a last resort, Charlotte decided to visit her father's half-sister, Helene Krabbe, whom she knew as Tante Leni, who was her guardian, who lived in Schwerin in Mecklenburg, some way from

Ludwigslust. Tante Leni had spent time with the family when the children were young, joining them on family outings in the car, as can be seen in the early family photographs.

Life with Tante Leni, 1940/41

Tante Leni Krabbe was a retired teacher, the oldest daughter of her father's first wife and half-sister to Andreas, Charlotte's father. Her appearance was that of an old-fashioned spinster. She wore flat shoes and unfashionable clothes, which were buttoned up to the neck. Because Charlotte was rather in awe of this aunt and once again needed moral support, she asked her friend Barbara to accompany her. They set off on a journey by train from Ludwigslust to Schwerin station, which is situated on the edge of a large lake. Charlotte and Barbara had to use their pocket money for the fare. Tante Leni lived right across the other side of the lake, away from the station, in an area known as the Lake District. It was a walk of some distance to reach her aunt's home. Charlotte had taken her friend along with her to give her courage to visit the aunt to ask if she could go to live with her. It was with some trepidation she asked her Tante Leni if she could have a home with her. She explained that Tante Lotti had said she must leave her and go to her stepmother. Although Tante Leni had often been on outings with her family while she was growing up it was a great surprise to Charlotte when her aunt said she could stay with her. Charlotte was aged about 14/15 when she moved to live with Tante Leni, whose home was in a block of flats. This was not long after her father's second marriage, and it would not be long also before he would die in March 1942.

The move to her Tante Leni's and Schwerin included a move to yet another school. While living at Tante Leni's,

Charlotte attended a girls' grammar school, which was close to her aunt's home. She felt she did not have opportunities to make friends at a school where friendships had already been made. Charlotte's disrupted education resulted in poor school reports while at the Schwerin Girls' Lyceum. She feels she educated herself by spending time reading in the library.

It turned out to be fortunate that other relatives had been unable to offer her a home because she was to have happy times with her old-fashioned maiden aunt, who proved to be very good company. Charlotte was surprised to find she had a wonderful time with her unglamorous aunt and that her aunt loved having her there. They had a good time together. There are many lakes near Schwerin, which is a picturesque area, and she and her aunt would take a boat on one of them. They visited museums, enjoyed cultural pursuits, and took an interest in botany. They would walk quite a distance to have Sunday lunch at the home of Onkel Hans Krabbe, a teacher, and Tante Margarete, who lived in a suburb of Schwerin.

Figure 24 Tante Leni with Ingeborg Mohr, née Meyer

Her cousin Ingeborg Meyer, who was already living with the aunt, had the spare bedroom, so Charlotte slept on a chaise longue in the dining room, with a window overlooking the garden. It was very hard and uncomfortable to lie on, and Charlotte could not get a good nights' sleep. Her feet used to dangle over the end of the chaise longue, which was not designed to be used as a bed, but it was worth putting up with that discomfort to be able to stay with her aunt. The flat's toilet and water were on a lower landing, so water had to be carried up in an ewer for them to wash themselves in a china bowl. A lower rent was charged for this flat as a consequence.

Although her Tante Leni hated swing band music, she let Charlotte have a little square radio to listen to the swing music she loved, as long as her aunt could not hear it. Charlotte had to hold the radio pressed to her ear, so she could listen to it quietly, so as not to disturb her aunt and only for an hour. Evidently, both Adolph Hitler and Joseph Goebbels hated swing music, but because it was popular with many people, they discovered it was very useful when used as a propaganda tool, and 'Charlie and his Orchestra' was the Nazi-sponsored German propaganda swing band. Radio broadcasts of it were made available to England, America, and Canada. It promoted Nazi slogans against the Jews, which were woven into the modified lyrics of well-known songs describing how Germany was defeating the allies. Who knows if Charlotte was absorbing these without understanding they were intended to spread Nazi ideology?

Vera Lynn was the forces' favourite in England, but Charlotte remembers that the Swedish singer Zarah Leander was a star, who sang to the German troops. But very popular with the German and allied soldiers of the Axis and allied troops was the song Lili Marlen, sung by Lale Andersen. She sang for Radio Belgrade. A later version of that love song was sung by Marlene Dietrich in 1944. It was another example of evocative music crossing language barriers.

After about six months, Charlotte's cousin Ingeborg left Aunt Leni's house to get married. Charlotte was able to escape the uncomfortable sofa, move into her cousin's former bedroom, and have a good night's sleep at last. She remembers it was heaven. Even though she had had such uncomfortable nights up until then, she thought it had been infinitely preferable to returning to live with her father and Erna, who was now her stepmother.

Another unusual happening, while living with Aunt Leni, was when her father Andreas unexpectedly visited. It seems he came especially to settle some payment. Tante Leni was his half-sister and he had been contributing an allowance to her of a generous sum of 27 Marks, paid monthly into a post office savings account. Charlotte did not know why he visited. She did not think it might be that he wanted to see her, but it would seem that he had her wellbeing at heart. While the payments continued, Tante Leni put aside the money she received, and as we shall see later, she too had Charlotte's wellbeing at heart. It was not long after this that Andreas entered a mental home, with early onset dementia. Charlotte thinks he may have seemed a little odd on the occasion of his visit. He had caught a train to Schwerin from Hanover rather than driving by car, and he had stopped off overnight in Hamburg on his way to see them. She could not account for these actions.

Charlotte managed to avoid attending BDM in her last year while at school in Schwerin. She had become aware there was political indoctrination, and she found that boring, so she escaped by keeping quiet and no one noticed. People who did not agree with the Nazis retreated by acquiescence into a quiet life. Charlotte said it was quite possible for anyone seen not to be in the party to be unable to get work.

Figure 25 Jürgen in the garden of Tante Lotti and Onkel Franz

Figure 26 Jürgen at Tante Lotti's

Charlotte describes with affection her brother Jürgen, who was tall and slim, with blond wavy hair and nice blue eyes. Charlotte said he was a lovely lad, who was popular with the girls. He was polite when a teenager and holidayed between the ages of 17 and 18 with groups going to the Alps and the seaside. He was musical, and to earn money, he worked as an extra at the Opera in Hanover and worked at night in the theatre in crowd scenes in costume saying 'rhubarb', 'rhubarb', 'rhubarb', to mimic indistinct conversation. Using rationed coupons, he bought socks and underwear and seasonal clothes, including a special jacket, of which he was particularly proud, which he wore when he visited Aunt Lotti. These would have been his more carefree days before Hitler appropriated his life.

Conscription, 1941

It was part of the natural progression when Jürgen left the Gymnasium ('grammar school') when he was 18 years old, for him to be conscripted straight into the army as a sergeant and sent to southern Germany to train. He later became a lieutenant adjutant of the 35th Panzer-Abteilung, with a 2nd-class Iron Cross. Members of the Hitler Youth were trained to be fed into the Wehrmacht (army), the German war machine. Jürgen, in his letters home, wrote that he was homesick. Charlotte said she did not appreciate what a difficult situation he was in, so did not write often, although she knew he would have liked more letters.

Figure 27 Jürgen in uniform

Death of Andreas, 1942

Charlotte was aged 15 and living at Tante Leni's when her father died, aged 56, in 1942 and she and Jürgen, who was aged 18, were orphaned. At the time their father died, he was living in a special home for people with dementia as he had early-onset dementia. Andreas appeared to be the victim of neglect while at the 'Paradise Care Home', in the Hildesheimer Straße, Hanover. Poor treatment there did not help his mental health, although it is said that his new wife, the former housekeeper, visited him regularly, and she said she took him food because he was ravenous and food was the main thing on his mind. Charlotte accompanied her on one occasion. She travelled by long-distance train from her home with Tante Lotti. Charlotte finds it is possible to imagine that Andreas may have been deliberately mistreated and starved to death. People with mental health problems could be disposed of in Nazi Germany. The mental health of Charlotte's father had deteriorated quite soon after he married Erna (6 September 1941), who inherited the family home and contents when he died on 29 March 1942 and was entitled to Andreas' pension. Charlotte thinks it not impossible that Erna might have persuaded Andreas to marry her when he was already showing signs of dementia. Erna soon remarried after he died, but her second husband also died, and it seems she married once more. Charlotte did not attend her father's funeral and does not know his last resting place even to this day because Erna would not tell her where her father was buried. Erna did not treat her son Klaus well, and later he would tell Charlotte he thought his mother was nasty.

In June 1941, Hitler had made a pact with Russia in order to invade Norway but instead invaded Russia and headed for Moscow. His intention was to repopulate all conquered territories with Germans by removing the people already living there. The Wehrmacht was only days away from Moscow when things did not progress as Hitler expected. The Battle of Barbarossa turned out to be a disaster, and the advance was stalled. Hitler made the same fatal mistake as Napoleon by causing his army units to endure a bitter, freezing Russian winter. The Russians had unexpectedly launched a counter offensive, and the Battle of Moscow, between December 1941 and January 1942, was during a winter that was the coldest of the 20th century, with temperatures as low as −45 degrees Celsius. Ill equipped German soldiers starved to death, and some froze to death whilst sleeping. The equipment and vehicles froze. By the end of 1941, there was destruction beyond belief, and the army was forced into retreat. Nevertheless, it appeared that Hitler was still confident of victory. And when the Japanese attack on Pearl Harbor on 7 December 1941, led to America declaring war on Japan, inexplicably, four days after that, Hitler declared war on America.

Figure 28 Jürgen relaxing at a house in Russia.

Charlotte said Jürgen had been sent towards Moscow after his training. He had told her they had been through Poland and taken it over. He said it was horrible. He may not have known that the Poles had had to endure invasion by the

Russian Army before that of the German army when Hitler broke his pact with Stalin. Jürgen said he did not like having to kill someone, but it had to be done. He told Charlotte he felt sorry for the Russians he was fighting because they were so very poor and uneducated, and were living in extremely poor conditions. We cannot know how much the soldiers in the Wehrmacht were ever aware that, in all of the Poland they were occupying, and elsewhere there were concentration camps and death camps, including that of Auschwitz, where over a million died. Similarly, we cannot tell whether they had any idea that from all countries occupied by Germany, millions of Jews and other 'undesirables' were being continually rounded up, put into rail trucks, and sent to the East to be killed, tortured, gassed, or starved in concentration and death camps. Perhaps they did not see or appreciate the wider picture beyond the system of which they were part while carrying out orders in a crazy world of atrocities. It would have been difficult for anyone not to be overwhelmed by the fear that they themselves might be killed by those giving the orders or by the enemy they were fighting on all fronts.

On their way eastwards, the Wehrmacht had attacked, set fire to, and destroyed villages and people as they went. They ate the locals' food, causing thousands to starve, and took anything that might be useful on their way through. When the tide turned and they had to retreat from the Russians, it was back through the areas already ravaged by war and with the Russians pursuing and attacking them, taking anything left to take. Everything in sight was ruined. One can well imagine the horror, fear, and despair experienced by the local families and their children and by all the other victims who were caught up in the conflict as both armies passed through. It would have been impossible for them to plant a crop for the next harvest. Charlotte mentioned that the oxen that would have pulled ploughs had been eaten. In the wasted countryside of the marshy area, with terrible narrow roads of thick mud, tanks became stuck and could not move forward. In the winter in the bitterly cold temperatures, the roads, which were in a terrible state, were made even worse when the snow thawed and they became almost impassable. Tanks and machinery broke down and were abandoned.

On one occasion, Charlotte met Jürgen at Tante Lotti's in Ludwigslust where he used to take his leave after their father died. He had been promoted to Lieutenant 3rd stage, with a shiny new hat as part of his new uniform. Because he did not want to stand out as newly promoted, he put the hat on a chair and asked Charlotte to sit on it to make it look as though it was well worn when he returned to his regiment. Charlotte said she loved doing things for him, but she was not so happy about his all black Panzer uniform. Jürgen would spend his last leave at Tante Lotti's. He hated having to go back to fight after his leave. He knew he might not survive. His job with the Panzers in the thick of the mayhem was to stay at the rear to protect the Germans when they were retreating. He said the Panzers were fighting against the up-to-date tanks of the Americans that had come through Murmansk. He told Charlotte that his understanding was that the German tanks were like sardine cans, easily pierced by the American army's new weapons.

Pflicht (Duty) Year at Domäne Dütschow

Figure 29 Pflicht year at Dütschow, 1942

Dütschow, 1942

In 1942, at the age of 16, Charlotte had to leave Tante Leni's and Schwerin. In Germany, from 1934–45, girls had to undertake a residential 'duty year', known as a *Pflichtjahr*. Charlotte had to choose between looking after children or working on a farm. As it happened, she went to the farm of Herr Schuster, who had children. It became her home for a year. It was near Hamburg on the River Elbe, called Domäne Dütschow, a tenant farm, consisting of farm buildings and about 100 acres in Dütschow. She said there are many little villages, mainly in North Germany, with names ending in the suffix -*ow*. Her duties included those of an au pair by looking after two children, whose mother was pregnant. One of the boys slept in Charlotte's bedroom, which was a bedsitting room. When the new baby was born, the second boy also shared Charlotte's room. The only means of transport available from the farm was by horse and cart.

Charlotte said she was careless about her belongings, and one day, one of the boys snatched her gold watch that was on her bedside table and threw it out of an open window that was above a part of the unused garden at the back of the house. Charlotte had inherited the gold watch from her mother and was very upset to lose it. The area it fell into was very deep in dead leaves, and the watch could not be found. Maybe it remains there to this day. Charlotte did not report its loss, although she felt so upset at losing her mother's watch, but once again, she made herself accept a situation she could not change. She was cross with the little boy, the oldest of the children, and does not know why he had acted that way. A new baby arrived before he was five, so he was quite young himself, perhaps making his naughtiness more understandable.

At the time, there were three children under five years of age to be looked after. Charlotte had to nurse two of the children when they were very ill with whooping cough, administering cold compresses and having them in bed with her. To keep their room warm, she had to heat the Kachelofen, a 'tiled stove' (masonry heater) that heated two rooms. A young cook, aged 16, had to rise early to make a fire in the kitchen range and then run with some of the fire to put in the stove in the children's room to heat it. It meant disturbed nights for Charlotte. Besides the young cook, there was a housemaid, who taught Charlotte how to do spring cleaning. In the afternoon, the farmer ordered the three of them to work in the garden. While the children were asleep, Charlotte had to work on the farm administration, and when the farmer, who was a Bürgermeister (mayor), was tired, he would send 16-year-old Charlotte to attend meetings on his behalf. He expected a lot of Charlotte, who said she had to work quite hard and felt resentful. Tante Leni would have complained on her behalf, but between them they decided she could cope and would adapt to the situation. She didn't like it much, but visiting her aunts on her free weekends helped her to put up with it. She was very glad to leave the family, once her year was up in 1943. It can be seen that, by the end of the Pflicht year, Charlotte had definitely learned the skills of a Hausfrau, but with extras.

In about 1942/43, in spite of the setback, the German army was continuing to attack the Russians and appeared to be invincible, but appearances had been deceptive. The battle for Stalingrad in southern Russia, between 23 August 1942 and 2 February 1943, changed everything. It resulted in two million casualties and Germany's catastrophic defeat, which stopped its advance into the Soviet Union when it surrendered in February 1943. Evidently, it was one of the bloodiest battles in the history of warfare. With a further horrific defeat at Kursk in July–August 1943, the Wehrmacht was now on the defensive. We now know that one of the contributory reasons for the Germans losing the Kursk battle was because the Russians had been warned by Bletchley Park of the planned German attack. Bletchley Park's code breakers had intercepted the plans of Hitler and his generals. Because of the easing of the Official Secrets Act, it is now known that this was partly thanks to the tireless work of Alan Turing, Tommy Flowers, and Bill Tutte amongst others, who played such a large part in defeating

Hitler. Ironically, they were the kind of men, including homosexuals and intellectuals, that Hitler despised. He would have got rid of them rather than nurturing their brilliance as was done in England.

The German army's position worsened even further that year in October 1943 when Italy switched sides to declare war on Germany. The Nazi army had now to fight those Italians who had turned to fight with the allies against the Germans. But some Italians continued to fight with the Germans, and the war was still far from over, and the continuation of the mass murder, atrocities, killings, and cruelty on an unimaginable scale went on.

Secretarial College and Tante Leni, 1943

During 1943, the year after her duty year, Charlotte, now aged 17, returned to live with Tante Leni at Schwerin in Mecklenburg while she attended a secretarial college. After spending six months at the college, Charlotte applied for a secretarial job on a farm at Banzin because Tante Leni had heard that the farm had a vacancy for a secretary.

Banzin – A New Life, 1943/4

Charlotte was aged about 17 when Tante Leni heard of a farmer who needed a secretary, and Charlotte became employed on the farm at Banzin that was situated in Mecklenburg, about 156 km northwest of Berlin, 62 km from Hamburg, and 140 km from Hanover.

Charlotte described a memorable occasion that happened when she used up some of her leave time from the farm at Banzin in order to visit Jürgen at Halle in the south, not far from Leipzig where he was stationed. It was a long journey for her by train via Hanover. Jürgen had two weeks' leave per year and occasional leave when he moved between training courses. On one occasion, early in his training, he invited Charlotte to go with him to the theatre at Halle in Saxony. He had managed to get three tickets, but one was separate, and it was a girlfriend that sat in the seat behind, while Charlotte and Jürgen sat together. It created a pleasant family experience for Charlotte, who remembers the occasion with great pleasure. It had made her feel special, for she and her brother had become companions, replacing their rivalry.

Banzin was situated in what Charlotte said was more a hamlet than a village. A new, eventful episode in her life was about to begin on the mixed farm, which was situated on good land of about 1,000 acres. The owner of the farm lived in a big castle-like house, and the tenant farmer and staff lived in the farmhouse. There were some experienced people remaining for the animal work. There were oxen, dairy cows, horses, pigs, piglets, and geese and hens. Crops mainly of barley and rye were also cultivated. Large quantities of vegetables were grown and sold for an hour a day to local people to raise an income. Charlotte was responsible for selling and delivering the vegetables. There were stables for the large animals, including oxen, and any cows and horses remaining there that had not been appropriated for the war effort. There was a pig man, someone in charge of the dairy, and another person responsible for ploughing besides the POWs and refugees residing on the farm, including the Poles. The POWs and refugees were taking the place of the civilians who had been conscripted into the Wehrmacht. They were probably part of the widespread slave labour that existed throughout Germany and its occupied countries, without which the Nazis could not have fed or financed the war. The only German civilians who remained working on the farm were the elderly and the very young. Until the final stages of the war, Charlotte had enough to eat, although it was plain food. At the farm, they had the benefit of refrigeration. It was in the form of blocks of ice, which were broken from the frozen lakes and kept in deep cellars. Charlotte spoke about walks on the Baltic for ice, which was delivered to the cities, including that which was delivered to her mother.

During the war, the increasing shortage of food, when people were starving, led to a black market. Charlotte considers that in Mecklenburg there was enough to eat, although food was in short supply. She said, when food was short, people ate whale meat or horseflesh when it was available. Charlotte thinks Tante Lotti took advantage of the fact that she knew all the shopkeepers in Ludwigslust personally, and she also went into the countryside to find food. But even she adjusted her behaviour to the circumstances created by the war's shortages. Charlotte explained that her corpulent aunt went strawberry picking. The strawberry pickers were partly paid in sugar, possibly 10 lbs, which was otherwise very scarce. It was a particularly hard task for Tante Lotti, who, because of her corpulence, had difficulty bending low enough to pick the strawberries. But it was a job worth doing because the strawberries could be made into conserves as well as eaten fresh. Charlotte marvels that, although there was no food, including sugar, available for the starving population, food in plenty was discovered at the end of the war, which had been stored in warehouses by the Nazis.

Because Banzin farm was in the countryside and Charlotte said that, living there, they were fortunate not to experience the effects of the war. They did not experience the bombing, although she became aware of what was happening elsewhere. Although the Banzin farm in Mecklenburg was insulated from the fighting and was some way distant from Hamburg, it experienced some of the effects of the mass bombing in which Hamburg was mainly destroyed in July1943. It was probably during Operation Gomorrah that a firestorm was created, whose smoke reached the farm and its soot settled on the washing that was hanging on the line. Evidently, the bombing caused many civilians to lose their lives and homes. Charlotte's relatives, including her two uncles and her Aunt Dabelstein, survived the bombing raid but lost their Hamburg homes when it was bombed in one of the relentless raids, causing them to move to rented rooms.

In winter, it was horrid at the farm, and Charlotte had what she has described as 'blue legs'. She had to rise early each day to supervise the feeding of the animals and oversee how much feed they were given. One of her tasks was to supervise the weighing of pigs to check they had not exceeded the stipulated maximum weight allotted for the acreage of the farm. People who were far distant from the farm gave the orders. The farmers were not allowed to overfeed their pigs, in order to avoid using up scarce food. Charlotte said that, while she was there, no one checked whether the task was done correctly because the civilians had been sent away to fight. Charlotte was a rebel, so made her own decisions. She had to sign a form when a farmer killed his own pig. She closed her eyes if they were larger than allowed because people liked fat in Germany. Everything was in a muddle, increasingly so as time went on, since the experts had left.

Another of Charlotte's tasks was to go by horse and cart to Vellahn station, which was five miles from the farm, to check addresses and complete the paperwork with the Stationmaster to make sure she did not get overcharged. The Government stipulated what should be grown on the farm and official orders stipulated the quantities of produce that were to be sent from the farm away to named destinations. These would have provided an important contribution to the war effort. Among Charlotte's various tasks was the booking of railway wagons. The produce was loaded onto the railway wagons, which could be open-sided or closed carriages.

On the farm, an old tractor with an engine fired by wood was utilized because there was no other fuel available for tractors or stoves. The chopping down of trees was forbidden except by official men who had permission. There were charcoal makers in the woods, who provided an important source of fuel.

Because Banzin was in the countryside, it was mostly unaffected by the massive bombing raids taking place in the cities and industrial sites around and afar in Germany. But it became a common sight for Charlotte to see American Super Fortress bombers passing over the farm so low that she could see the bombs hanging beneath. She said it was so horrifying to see them.

The farm could not have defended itself if it had been attacked, but the planes they saw were on their way to bomb Berlin or other targets. Even Ludwigslust was spared the bombing except for the occasion when the bomber had jettisoned its load of bombs away from its original target, causing some damage to Tante Lotti's house.

On one of her free weekends from the Banzin farm, Charlotte visited her two aunts. It was possible to visit both on the same day by train. She took with her a chicken she intended to give to Tante Leni after calling at Tante Lotti's in Ludwigslust on the way there. When she left her Aunt Lotti's to catch the train to reach Tante Leni's, in Schwerin, Charlotte completely forgot to take the chicken with her, which had been put in a cool place, so was startled to hear someone calling her name from the platform. Her very corpulent aunt was running and out of breath in her hurry to catch up with Charlotte. She was carrying in her arms the forgotten, unwrapped chicken with its legs dangling. Her aunt almost threw the chicken through the train carriage window to the embarrassment of the 18/19-year-old Charlotte and the amazement of the other passengers. The passengers were at first annoyed because they were envious of the chicken, which would have been a rare treat for them, but then they were good-humoured and saw the funny side of it. Her aunt, though corpulent, was always well dressed and always looked elegant. Charlotte said she felt guilty that she had caused her aunt to run because she could have had a heart attack. When Charlotte got off the train at Schwerin station, she was met on that occasion by Tante Leni. Her aunt accompanied her on the long walk round the lake to her home.

The railways were kept in surprisingly good order, and the train service was really efficient all through the war up until the very last days. The trains were still running well for her journeys that weekend and the timetables reliable. Charlotte said the lines were repaired continually after they had been bombed.

While living at the farm, Charlotte had a friendship with a boy, who, she said, was not a boyfriend. The two used to tease each other on the phone, but she warned him she was not in love with him. They met once and cycled together. It was awkward, and she felt embarrassed. It was not romantic. But someone was about to enter her life, with whom she would feel the opposite of uncomfortable.

Romance, 1943/44

Charlotte received a letter from her brother Jürgen in about 1943, whilst he was training, in which he wrote to tell Charlotte about his friend Manfred Kurz, whom he had met when training at Bamberg in Franconia. He told her he would be coming to near where she was and suggested she should go and visit him.

Summer 1944

Manfred and Charlotte became pen friends, and after exchanging many letters, their friendship developed into a romance, and the young officer, who was three years older than her, became her boyfriend, and they wished to meet. Charlotte arranged to visit Manfred whilst he was training at the Officer Training Camp at Bergen. Situated on the Lüneburg Heath in Lower Saxony, it was the largest military training camp in Germany. To provide Charlotte with an excuse to visit Manfred, the farmer's wife at Banzin had provided Charlotte with some food and a chicken to take with her, so she could stay at the home of the farmer's wife's aunt. The aunt happened to live near the training camp. In the summer of 1944, aged about 17/18, Charlotte set off on a journey. Because she had to change trains on the way there, it took two hours to get to the aunt's house in Bergen, but Charlotte was looking forward to the new experience.

Figure 30 Charlotte and Manfred, summer 1944

She stayed at the home of the farmer's aunt's for a weekend. She wore her one and only dress with its special velvet belt. She said the dress was easy to wash and did not crease. It was lovely, wonderful summer weather, and she liked Manfred as soon as she saw him. He was tall and so handsome. When he called for her, she experienced what was for her the most romantic time in her life. There were few distractions because the training camp on the Lüneburg heathland of sandy soil and heather was miles from anywhere. In the lovely warm sunshine, they walked through the fields of rye, which had grown higher than their heads. It was possible to walk and stop and rest completely out of view. The rye, which was grown for the bread that all Germans ate, had not at that time undergone the modern farming practices that later would produce the shorter-stemmed rye. In the sun, the rye smelt pungently, and the unspoilt fields were full of poppies, cornflowers, and marguerites, and the birds were singing. It was all so natural, and they felt easy in each other's company, confirming her romantic feelings for him. Everything about it was so romantic. The memories of that time they spent together on that special occasion still remain as a warm memory in a special part of Charlotte's heart. They would wish to meet again.

In the background of this wonderful wartime romance, unbeknown to Charlotte and Manfred when he showed her round the Bergen Officers Training camp, where he was based, there was another large complex nearby. It was largely hidden from the outside world behind large, barbed-wire enclosures, which Charlotte saw close to the training camp, but she saw no sign of buildings or people or that it had a special purpose. She finds it hard to understand how neither she nor Manfred could be so close to it and yet be totally unaware of its sinister history. But she said that hidden suspicious-looking places were suspected of being where experimental top-secret new and advanced weapons were being invented to use against England. The fences were so constructed that no one could climb into them or climb out of them.

But if she had been in this vicinity some months after her romantic visit to Manfred, she would have witnessed many thousands of emaciated prisoners being herded into the Bergen-Belsen concentration camp by the Nazi guards. They were among so many, who were force-marched hundreds of miles by guards, trying to remove them from camps of all kinds in the East, which were being approached by the Soviet Army. The guards were attempting to remove the evidence of the dreadful treatment they had perpetrated on innocent people. It has been suggested that it was to ensure that the prisoners could not be liberated. Although she saw nothing at that time, some months later, we shall see, Charlotte was not spared.

Life on the Banzin Farm, 1943–45

Back home on the farm at Banzin, there were twenty Russian POWs, who did not have a nice life, but it could have been even worse for them elsewhere. Because Russia had not signed the Geneva Convention, they received no outside support, and they did not receive Red Cross parcels. The Slavs did receive parcels and were looked on favourably, and in payment for their socks being darned by Charlotte, they gave her bars of toilet soap from their parcels. She was good at darning and used specialist wool, which she held in store, which previously had not been needed. Many thousands of prisoners besides these at Banzin, including those from all the occupied countries, were forced to labour for the Germans. Many were working in the armament factories in dreadful conditions. Their work would continue for the duration of the war. One of the Slavs at the farm was named Radic. We shall hear of him again. Some of those who were labouring elsewhere were virtually slaves. Some possibly did not mind being at Banzin, where life, may have been bearable, in comparison to what they might have endured elsewhere. Millions of prisoners were treated extremely badly by the Germans and lived in the harshest of conditions until they were too frail to be of any use and either died of hunger or exhaustion or were murdered. At the farm, there were examples from several nationalities, including Serbs, Slavs, Russians, Poles, and French.

Russians were singled out for payment at a very low rate for their work, and the only food they were given were potatoes. They ate these in an annex in the farmhouse in the daytime. Charlotte was amazed to see that they were washed and boiled in a big container with their skins on and nothing added to them. Charlotte said she was horrified when she saw that the cooked potatoes boiled in a big copper boiler heated by a fire, were drained and poured onto a wooden table and the Russians ate them with their fingers because they had no cutlery. She learned from her brother Jürgen that this was not an uncommon occurrence amongst people who lived in very poor parts of Russia.

At first, Charlotte was scared of the Russian soldiers and felt no sympathy for them. She said that Hitler's propaganda had filled people with fear with tales of the Russians' brutality and what they would do to women. But as their uniforms became worn and shabby, she began to pity them. There was only one elderly guard because these Russians were not perceived as a threat at this time. One of Charlotte's tasks was to go alone with the Russian POWs to the barn where they shovelled animal food onto scales and then into sacks, ready to be taken to the station. The prisoners were scared to return to Russia. Those who did were sometimes shot on Stalin's orders, possibly for allowing themselves to be taken prisoner. Millions of slave labourers were used to keep the war effort going.

Daily life in Germany became composed of shortages and hunger. Soap was not readily available for the laundry, which was washed by hand. Charlotte said that, in order to avoid contracting fleas, soap was made in a washtub. Animal fat from animal bones with chemicals added was poured into big washtubs and when it set it was cut into squares. It was not at all pleasant, in fact, it was horrible. When an aunt of the farmer came to visit there was a rumour that she had brought some real soap with her. It was considered such a rare treat that it excited comment, and they all wanted to smell its fragrance, and all went in her room to have a surreptitious sniff. All German industry was geared towards war, so it was difficult for anyone to buy everyday items, including cutlery and clothes. There was no leather available for shoes.

Charlotte had to give up her nice, large downstairs room at the farm for a smaller room, to make room for a German family, who were refugees from East Prussia, where they had lost their homes. She was sad to lose it. Three Polish families, including children, were living over the pigsties at the farm at Banzin. They had been forcibly brought to the farm to work because there was a need for workers as German men were away in the war. Charlotte said they did not mind being at the farm, where they were warm and fed, although they were only paid a pittance by the farmer. Charlotte visited the Poles in the loft to pay them. She said conditions in there were quite smelly, so she did not like going up. The Polish children received no education and had to help with the farm work. There were Serbs, too, at the farm, who also did not wish to go back home.

Among all her duties, Charlotte was also responsible for looking after the timesheets of the workers of the different nationalities.

The various nationalities were paid different rates and soon complained if Charlotte made mistakes in her calculations. Two French POWs were among the many nationalities that found themselves at the farm. They were trusted to work for a couple of other farmers, which was surprising to Charlotte because she thought it would have been easier for them to escape from there to their home areas. But unbeknown to her, life in occupied France and under the Vichy government was not without its own dangers. Jews, for instance, learned to their dismay that they were not safe when thousands were deported to the death camps from France in cattle trucks, which had no facilities and in which they endured appalling conditions on their way to the gas chambers.

I asked Charlotte whether she had learned from the various prisoners and arrivals at the farm about the experiences they had been through, but it seems she did not. She said she did not understand the languages of the Slavs or the Poles. She seems to have accepted the very strange situation she found herself in without questioning the presence of the various nationalities. She had accepted it as all part of a wartime experience. We now know that the German economy was kept going by the industry and work of slave labourers from occupied countries who, unlike those working at Banzin, experienced lives that were very far from being good.

The father of Charlotte's friend Barbara, who was the former Luftwaffe officer so badly injured in the First World War, had said he wanted the war to finish and wanted assassination plots to succeed. We now know that one attempt almost did.

Jürgen and Charlotte said the soldiers did not wish to be in the war, but, as part of the army, they followed instructions. It seems they talked of overthrowing Hitler after the war, but Hitler survived several assassination attempts. He spent much of his time protected in what was known as the fortified Wolf's Lair, hiding and plotting with his henchmen between 1941 and 1944. There were at least six attempts on Hitler's life. But it seems that, for a while, he gained even more support after failed attempts on his life. Then, the final attempt with a bomb in a suitcase in his Wolf's Lair bunker in East Prussia also failed on 20 July 1944. A table leg bore the brunt of the timed bomb blast, and although other people in the room were hurt and Hitler too, he survived. Hitler must have felt invincible. An injured

Hitler had the assassination plotters Claus von Stauffenberg and his allies executed. After removing those responsible for the attempt on his life, he surrounded himself with those on whom he thought he could rely to follow his orders. He only abandoned the Wolf's Lair as late as 20 November 1944 to go to Berlin when forced by the imminent arrival of the Red Army in East Prussia. The last four months of his life, from 16 January 1945, were spent in the Führerbunker in Berlin, where, unhappily, his reign of terror continued.

Charlotte was unaware that, miles away, a summer offensive, known as Operation Bagration, took place from 29 June 1944 to 3 July 1944. The Red Army had encircled the Germans who were defending in Belarus, but Hitler's orders were that there must be no retreat. It was to be defended at all costs. The Germans in Minsk were completely encircled by Soviet troops. They were facing overwhelming odds. Two German field marshals travelled to appeal to Hitler in person, in order to save unnecessary loss of life, but Hitler commanded those in charge to continue to defend. The result was that most of the encircled German army units were killed and were shattered within a matter of days when Minsk was recaptured by the Soviet troops in July. Thousands of Germans and Russians died. The Germans had endured attacks from the air and land, and by tanks. All the horrors of warfare were taking place in vast swathes of Belarus and the Ukraine as the Germans retreated and defended while under constant attack. This was not only from the Russians but also the partisans, who were causing major disruptions. By autumn 1944, the German's were in retreat. As far as Stalin was concerned, it seems life was cheap. Many times, Hitler ordered the army to fight, however impossible the situation. It seems life was cheap as far as he was concerned too.

The significance of this for Charlotte was that Minsk was the furthest East that her brother Jürgen had been sent. His job in the Panzers was to defend the unit as it retreated. Jürgen had told Charlotte that, once the Americans arrived, the game changed for them. He said they could not hope to win against the American tanks, which were brought over the arctic to Murmansk. He said he felt as though he was in a sardine can, which could be easily pierced. The Germans were ill equipped, and Jürgen had said that there was not enough ammunition. Charlotte's opinion was that it was never a Nazi army. She described it as an old-fashioned army, directed by Nazis.

Jürgen's Death, July 1944

Figure 31 Jürgen, June 1944

Jürgen in his Panzer Regiment had by this time been in the war for two and a half years. He said they had been through Poland and taken it over. The Wehrmacht had made a push forward to within a fairly short distance of Moscow, but the Russians unexpectedly turned the tide. The Russians began to have successes against the German Wehrmacht, which was stretched all along the eastern front. Jürgen said his Panzer unit had been ordered to support the retreating army rather than attacking. Sadly, in his last letter to Charlotte, Jürgen complained that she wrote less to him after she began writing to Manfred, the friend to whom he had introduced her. She replied to his letter straightaway, but she does not know if her letter got to him because she did not hear from him ever again.

It was about this time, that Charlotte took some of her leave from the farm during the Summer of 1944 to meet her boyfriend Manfred. Manfred who was the recipient of a first-class Iron Cross medal. She went to stay with him in the Black Forest area. It was a day's journey away from the farm. She travelled to Hamburg, where she changed trains to meet Manfred at his home in Freiburg, to which he had gone to fetch his suitcase. He introduced Charlotte to his mother and brother. His parents were divorced. I think she said Manfred wanted to hurry to where he had booked rooms in a Pension, a small hotel in the beautiful scenic area of the Black Forest. It was positioned at the meeting point of Germany, Switzerland, and France in an area renowned for its woodcarving and cuckoo clocks. It was a beautiful, peaceful, and quiet walking area where they spent their time walking on the typically waymarked footpaths, returning to the pension for lunch and evening meals. Charlotte felt at that time that the war was going well, but appearances can be deceptive, for in 1944 and even earlier, the Germans were suffering defeats, and German soldiers were surrendering. All was definitely not going well.

Then, after a long though uneventful journey home from the Black Forest, Charlotte received some devastating news when she got off the train at Vellahn.

Bad News, July 1944

Charlotte's best schoolfriend, Barbara Lorenz from Ludwigslust, whose own brother had been killed in the war when he was aged 18, had called at the Banzin farm to give Charlotte some news but was directed instead to the station to meet Charlotte. Barbara had unwelcome news about Jürgen, which Aunt Lotti had asked her to pass on to Charlotte. She drove the horsedrawn cart to meet her from the station at Vellahn. There, she gave Charlotte the news that her brother Jürgen, who was aged 20, had been killed on 10 July 1944. It had taken Charlotte over a day to make the return journey to Vellahn from the Black Forest. She was tired after her journey but had still been feeling happy because she had seen Manfred. The news from Tante Lotti, however, changed everything. Barbara took her back to the farm where Charlotte changed and repacked her suitcase then caught a train to Tante Lotti's who, as next of kin, had received the official letter. There, she and her aunt cried together. Charlotte said she felt very hurt that her aunt expressed the thought that Jürgen's death marked the end of the family. She felt she was not valued because she was not a boy because boys were the ones considered important in Germany. Charlotte felt that her aunt did not realize she was not the only one who was sad. She did not sympathize or recognize Charlotte's sadness. Charlotte felt it seemed as though she was cross with her and was upset that she had received no sympathy.

Jürgen was aged only 20 when he died on 10 July 1944 fighting on the Eastern Front. He was killed by artillery fire in Slonim, Belarus, although he was not in the front line. The German tank units, including his, had been ordered to protect the German army, which was retreating under fire. The Panzers had to form a barrier and had been specially chosen to stay behind to defend the retreating units. According to the Volksbund, Jürgen died at Slonim and was buried at Zelva in Belarus. The intention was for bodies to be repatriated post-war. Charlotte has not wanted to visit his grave. She says flowers would die, he would not be there, and she would not wish to see his among so many sad graves. Charlotte was only 18 years old.

By late 1944, when Germany was facing allied armies to the west and six million fighting in the Soviet army to the East, when allied planes were almost constantly bombing and levelling cities, including Berlin, in air raids, Hitler was at briefings. Norman Ohler, in his book 'Blitzed', suggested that the records from 1936 of Hitler's personal doctor, Theodor Morrell, indicate that Hitler, at this precarious time, was taking much medication and was addicted to steroids and opioids. He maintains also that Hitler, in the last months of the war, was taking more and more cocaine until no more supplies could be acquired for him. There are many theories about Hitler's health and state of mind. But there would need to be an autopsy and scientific analysis to confirm or disprove the theories. Meanwhile, Germany continued on its path of self-destruction, a path dictated by someone who appears to have lost all sense of reality.

October 1944

It became obvious that the war in Germany was falling apart. Great numbers of soldiers attempted to desert, although there were orders that those who tried to leave would be shot. By that time, Germany was being attacked on all sides. In order to increase numbers to fight, Hitler and the Nazi party created the Volkssturm ('people's storm'), an untrained civilian army. Young boys and even old men were forced into the army. Some were without uniforms or equipment, with only an armband to identify them as soldiers. Many would become cannon fodder, but others would fight on ferociously. Among them was the owner of the farm, as well as the tenant farmer who was Charlotte's employer. He was horrified when, in about October 1944, he was ordered to leave the farm, leaving his wife and Charlotte to run it in his absence. Charlotte said she had no idea how to run a farm. Also as a consequence of the farmer's leaving, she became responsible for his Banzin mayoral duties at the age of 18 years. The farmer, who was Bürgermeister, had handed over the office to her. She said all villages had mayors. These duties were added to those of her farm secretary work in the last few months of the war. One of her tasks was to give out ration cards, of which she said there was a large supply. Sometimes, she secretly gave out double ration cards to soldiers on leave, although this was against the rules. No one knew what was going on. Today, from a distance, it all seems bizarre.

Part of Charlotte's mayoral duties was the weighing of pigs from other farms that were about to be killed. Except for the tail, every part of the pig was used, including the blood, used for the making of black sausage. The pigs were not to exceed a stipulated weight, for that would have indicated that they had been given more than the stipulated amount of feed. Charlotte said she made generous allowance. The pigs were stunned before their throats were cut to allow the blood to be caught and saved for the making of black sausage. The black sausage was one of many kinds eaten in Germany. They were displayed hygienically behind glass and are still made today. In peacetime, the various types were eaten at the evening meal on slices of dark bread and butter with an assortment of cold sausage and cold tongue. Chopped tongue and white fat were included in its recipe as well as spices and seasoning. Charlotte said she managed to avoid weighing her farm's own pigs, and they were never checked. She said she loved the piglets, and they were always clean. One of her tasks was to count her farm's piglets to give the numbers to the accountant. It was an impossible task because they did not stand still, and sometimes, pigs had mysteriously disappeared.

Charlotte's Weekend Breaks

While living at the farm at Banzin, Charlotte made friends with the wife of a forester, whose husband had been in charge of the forests. He was among those forced to go off to fight in the last year of the war when Germany was losing and needed reinforcements. His wife was left to live alone in the middle of the forest, so on some weekends, Charlotte went to keep her company and experienced a different way of life without home comforts. She stayed the night because the farm was too distant to cycle back to in a day. The enormous bedrooms were like fridges. It became an endurance test in winter when the temperatures dropped at night and it was time for Charlotte and her friend to climb into their beds, which were so very cold. But eventually, the heavy duvet, which may have contained duck down, became cosily warm. So much so that getting out of bed in the morning was another ordeal to be endured. This was especially so because there was no running water in the house and the water in a washbowl and pitcher had frozen overnight. Charlotte spent several weekends with her because they had become friends.

A Leap to Save Her Life

At about this stage in the war, Charlotte was on her way on the 45-minute journey to Vellahn Station in the horsedrawn cart to see the stationmaster when suddenly an English plane passed overhead and she could see its pilot, who also saw her. She could see the plane's English marking clearly. She shook her fist at him, but then he turned the plane and, to her great fright, began shooting at her with a machine gun. She feels he must have seen she was a woman. Her horse went wild, spinning the cart round and round in its terror, so Charlotte threw herself into a ditch under a hedge until eventually the horse calmed down and returned to wait for her. Amazingly, she was not hurt, though the tree and branches in the hedge covering the ditch in which she was hiding showed signs of damage from the shooting. She was relieved that the plane did not turn back again. Charlotte was not hurt but was badly shaken, and when all was quiet again, she climbed back onto the cart, and she and the horse completed their journey to the station. There, she completed the relevant paperwork with the stationmaster. This was during the time that Charlotte had been left to run the farm with the farmer's wife. The episode was a great shock to Charlotte because, in spite of seeing the American bombers heading for their destinations to attack major targets further away, they felt isolated at Banzin and safe from the fighting, which was taking place on all fronts and from the air against the Germans. But at about the same time, the wife of the owner of the farm also experienced an attack and was wounded when she was on a train that was machine-gunned by English planes. Charlotte said the train was an easy target because it was surrounded by farmland without defence in the form of artillery.

The actual fighting was now getting too close to Charlotte for her comfort.

Sometime before the end of the war, people in the cities were literally starving, and Charlotte described how people sold their jewellery and valuables for food to black marketeers or swapped them for food. Cigarettes had a high value. Although people in the cities were starving, on the farms it seems they were more fortunate, for there were chickens and eggs and milk, from which the cream had been removed, but even so, on the farm at Banzin they were still hungry. Charlotte explained that she had her main meal in the middle of the day, and she was lucky to have it, but by evening, several hours later, she was very hungry again. Although eating milk soup made her wretch at first, she said there was no alternative but to persuade herself to like it. The milk soup was made from creamy milk from the farm's own cows, in which a handful of flour was beaten up and kept overnight to thicken. No sugar was added, but it was nutritious. Even in peacetimes, she said, milk soup was widely eaten in Germany. By March 1945, there was no food left unless they cheated. At the farm, food shortages had not been serious until late in the war.

War-time rations in Germany consisted of 2 oz butter per week, but it varied. Usually, there were potatoes and bread. In earlier times, produce such as butter and bread had been sold at the farm for an hour a day or exchanged for vegetables. It had been a kind of minimarket. Small piglets were sold when there was nothing with which to feed them.

Blueberry Treat, Summer 1944

Because there was so little food available, there is another especially pleasant day that Charlotte looks back on and treasures in her memory. She remembers going with others into the countryside in July. It became a special day because they gathered the Blueberries growing in the heathland. Everyone at the farm took bowls and travelled by lorry to help pick the blueberries. Because the blueberry bushes grew close to the ground, the task of filling great churns with the berries was back-aching work, especially as the task took a whole day. At the end of the back-aching day, the pickers were rewarded with a bowl of blueberries and milk and even some of the sugar ration. Charlotte said it was delicious.

During the last months of the war, a contingent of about 200 Polish officers turned up at Banzin. They had been brought from a camp under guard. It is possible they were being taken to Belsen. They turned up at the farm and bedded down for the night. There was not even straw or hay for them by then, but they used some salvaged bits of straw to make slippers to barter for food. Charlotte said they had not washed so were smelly. The men stayed in a barn or an empty hayloft. Charlotte said that on the farm, they had no food to give. It is unlikely the prisoners would have any idea of the destination they were being herded to only that it was away from a Poland of ill-treatment, concentration camps, and ravaged countryside. Even before the outbreak of war, Polish officers had been killed on Stalin's orders in a notorious act. But then, Hitler marched into Poland, and that became the start of the Second World War. Hitler would soon put into action the mass murder of Jews and civilians in what was termed the 'Final Solution'.

The Final Solution

It is often said, and by many people , that the German population must have known something about the attempted wholesale genocide of the Jews and other outcasts including gypsies and homosexuals. They were just a small example from a long list of those who would detract from Hitler's ideals of a super race. It is asked how could people not be aware? Charlotte said that she for one did not know of it.

She said the farm at Banzin, where she started her new job in 1943, was away from everything. She said that, although there were camps, which were heavily fortified with barbed wire, it was impossible for anyone to see what was happening inside. This was the case when she was unknowingly near the Bergen Belsen camp with Manfred, where there was no sign of its purpose to the outside world. She said her aunts at Ludwigslust and Schwerin were suspicious that something illegal was going on in such fortified places. She said they had thought it was something political to do with the war. And she said there were what she called whispers. People preferred to bury their heads in the sand. It seems that, if some news of the dreadful treatment in the camps trickled out, it simply served to increase people's fear of being arrested. It was fear that gave the Nazis the power to keep control. An enormous number of camps were located away from civilisation. A great many death camps were in Poland, but on one day, a day she will never forget, Charlotte was brought face to face closer to home with some of the innocent victims of the Nazi Regime and of man's inhumanity to man. What she saw that day was actually a very tiny sample of what was reality for literally millions of the unwanted people who detracted from the Nazi ideal, but it was no less horrific for that. Her eyes were forced opened by the shock of what she saw, and she gained just an inkling of the atrocities that were being orchestrated by Hitler, aided and abetted by his willing and enthusiastic henchmen on a scale absolutely impossible to imagine.

It was possibly in about March 1945, very close to the end of the war, when Charlotte had the horrific experience that opened her eyes to what had previously been invisible. She was cycling alone from the farm along the main road between Hamburg and Berlin to the pharmacy at Banzin. The road was quiet because of lack of petrol for vehicles when she became aware of an awful stench. That was the first thing she noticed, and she cannot forget it even today. She saw coming towards her a horrific, ghastly sight. It was of a group of emaciated men and women who looked more like skeletons than people. They did not look human. A woman guard at the front and an old feeble soldier at the rear, with a gun slung over his shoulder, were supposedly guarding the men and women prisoners, who, she thinks, numbered about 30. Charlotte said hello, but no one answered. They kept their heads down. It was a complete shock. She said she cycled past as fast as she could. She can recall their smell even today. At that time, she just wanted to escape it. She felt embarrassed and could not bear to look at the prisoners. It is unlikely they would have had enough strength to attempt to escape, and in any case, where could they go? It was usual for any stragglers or prisoners who attempted to escape to be shot by SS guards.

Charlotte said that, because of the imminent threat of the Russians drawing ever closer to the farm, she was at this time too preoccupied with the problems of her own precarious situation to dwell on what she saw that day on her way to the pharmacy in Banzin, although the image and the smell coming from it remain with her to this day. Charlotte said she did not know where the emaciated prisoners whom she saw that day were being moved from or to where they were being moved, but she now thinks they must have been en route to Bergen-Belsen. Charlotte, like the rest of the world, learned that this group of prisoners was an infinitesimal example of the brutal treatment and cruelty being meted out to millions of people who were considered by Hitler, Himmler, Göring, and Goebbels among other leading Nazis not to be human or worthy of life.

By that time, prisoners were being forced to walk hundreds of miles from the Holocaust concentration camps in the East to prison camps in Germany to keep them out of sight of the liberating armies. Many were too weak to survive the journeys or were murdered en route. Gypsies, Slavs, Jews, resistance workers, and political opponents are only a few of the examples from a long list of people subjected to inhuman treatment because they were deemed suitable for death or exploitation on an unimaginable scale. The Polish officers who had turned up at the farm at Banzin were possibly part of this large-scale movement of victims.

In 1945, it was as early as 27 January, that soldiers of the Soviet army unexpectedly discovered, on entering Auschwitz Birkenau in Poland, a sight so horrific that it could have affected the mental health of those who saw the extent of the horrors that had taken place in there. Any effort to erase all evidence of the crimes committed there had failed.

A few months after this, on 15 April 1945, the British troops also discovered an horrific sight deep in a wooded area close to Manfred Kurz's former training camp at Bergen. It was the notorious Bergen-Belsen concentration camp, a death camp. Belsen was initially intended as a work camp, but thousands more prisoners were forced into it, causing chronic overcrowding, resulting in disease and starvation on an unimaginable scale, with thousands of dead and dying. There was nothing at all for them to eat. It is possible to conjecture that it might have included the prisoners Charlotte had seen on the road near the farm at Banzin if any had managed to survive the cruel journey. Once in the camp, they would have endured death by neglect and starvation and ill treatment, like so many others. Their only crime was they were considered by the Nazis to be inferior and enemies of the state or of no use. The English who liberated the Belsen camp took on the humanitarian crisis, although the war was still raging around them. They made the people of Bergen physically confront the reality of the scale of cruelty perpetrated in their midst, though people protested that they had not known what had been going on so close to home.

As I mentioned before, it is difficult to accept the truth that the Belsen camp of horrors was situated next door to the Officer Training camp where Charlotte had visited Manfred and had experienced her most moving wartime romance without either Manfred or herself being aware of what was taking place close by. Charlotte finds it hard even now to accept that truth.

Burning of Documents

Charlotte mentioned how in 1945, in the same way that there were attempts to hide the physical signs of the atrocities meted out to millions, once it was seen that the war was lost, there was also much burning of documents throughout the countries that had been occupied during the Third Reich in order to hide them. But in his book entitled *The SS Officer's Armchair*, author Daniel Lee describes how at least one SS officer had hidden his documents in the upholstered seat of a chair rather than burning them. Many years after the war, these were unexpectedly brought to light, giving in great detail the orders he implemented each day without a thought of the suffering he was causing to innocent people. The officer's daughters were astonished to learn about the part he played in the smooth running of the Third Reich and the Holocaust. He was playing his role at the same time and within the same home as his two daughters were living with him. The sisters expressed very different emotions from each other. They expressed either disbelief or did not care. His part in the success of the Holocaust was only one part of so many doing the same thing throughout Germany, who were aiding the whole system to function and achieve Hitler's plan. They were all cogs in a bureaucratic killing machine.

In February or March 1945, Himmler was still issuing orders to help rid the world of Jews. These continued right up until the last possible opportunity, even though the German army was retreating and in some areas totally surrendering. The rounding up and killing of Jews or anyone who did not fit the Aryan profile was to continue. It is hard to grasp why Himmler felt it was his duty. He firmly believed in the need for the Holocaust to cleanse the German race, and unbelievably, like Goebbels Himmler felt no remorse right up to his suicide by cyanide poisoning after his capture by the allies. He felt he had done the right thing in helping to purify the nation of undesirables. And his evil instructions resulted in people being killed until the last available moment when they could have been allowed to survive. He has been described as the quintessential Nazi, a coldblooded mastermind of genocide. His troops showed a fanaticism and devotion to Hitler.

In the last months of the war, everything in Germany that had been in good order was being neglected. No one knew what was going on. Hitler had retreated into his bunker in the Reich Chancellery, preferring to ignore reality. He was issuing orders, which people continued to follow, although they would have known the situation was impossible. Such was the power he had over them. Hitler was still determined that against all odds Berlin should continue to be defended against the Russians, who were approaching a city that was also under constant attacks by American and

English bombers and armies on all sides. Hitler was supported by Albert Speer, the Minister of Armaments and War Production, who was encouraged to deliver more and more armaments, including the V-2 rocket, which was to be constructed by the slave labourers of occupied countries. Right up until the surrender, the imprisoned labourers were building the instruments of war that would be rained on their own countries. It seems Speer supported and admired Hitler as much as Goebbels, Himmler, and Göring did. It seems to have been a sort of hero worship.

From about September 1944 until at least March 1945, the Nazis were launching V-2 Rockets from mobile rocket launchers against European cities. This continued to cause death and destruction in Europe's cities, including London. The rockets, known colloquially as doodlebugs, dropped silently, giving no warning, which made them more sinister and unnerving. There was no way of intercepting these mobile attacks, which could be launched from anywhere.

Charlotte's Brave or Rash Decision

At about the end of March 1945, when news of the war's situation was becoming dire, Charlotte received word that Manfred had been injured and was recuperating at a military hospital for officers. The convalescent home was near the Czech border with the Sudetenland, somewhere far from the theatre of war. Manfred had been fighting the Russians in the East in Poland, and by that time, the German army was on the defensive in many areas but continuing to attack fiercely in others. On hearing the news, Charlotte immediately left the farm without asking for leave. She said she felt apprehensive and frightened, but she thought the railways were in good order so would go to him. It was rather a reckless decision at that stage in the fighting with the enemy so close, but she set off on a long and hazardous journey from one end of Germany to the other to visit him. It was a day's journey away—a journey that skirted a Berlin that was under constant attack. The trains she travelled on were old and a far cry from the usual high standard. It was clear that everything in Germany was noticeably falling apart.

Her journey took her not too far from Dresden, which had been bombed on 13–15 February 1945 by English and Americans. The bombing was a controversial decision because, by that time, it was obvious to all that the Germans were losing the war. Millions of citizens were killed in the raids, and little of Dresden was left standing. Charlotte is of the opinion that Dresden was bombed because it contained many refugees who had fled from the Russians and were gathered there from the East. But other observers dispute that. But it is probably true that refugees had thought that, as it was near the border, it would be safe since the war was seen to be nearly over.

Charlotte saw Manfred, his head dressed with a white bandage, when he met her off the train at a tiny station. He had booked rooms at a nice hotel for bed and breakfast on the Czech border in a beautiful area, which was almost empty of people. In peacetime, it would have been busier as it was a favourite holiday spot in the Erzgebirge Mountains. Known as the Ore Mountains, it is now a World Heritage Site. It had been a favourite of Charlotte's Onkel Franz, a biologist, because it was unspoilt. He used to go there on his own. Through her bedroom window at night, Charlotte heard the trickle of the mountain stream's water behind her hotel room. It was idyllic, very peaceful, and astonishingly, totally untouched by the war, except for the presence of the wounded with their bandaged heads. Charlotte saw other soldiers who, it seems, mainly had head wounds. Where they were recuperating, it was as if there were no war. Charlotte thinks the wounded soldiers were in no hurry to get back to the fighting and were staying there as long as they could.

Charlotte and Manfred, who were very much in love, spent their time alone, sight-seeing and walking in the mountains, following the clearly waymarked mountain trails and visiting restaurants for meals where there was still food available. Then, one evening, when they arrived back at the hotel, they were astonished to find that, although it was not late, the front door was locked. None of the guests came to let them in when they knocked on the door. Fortunately, Charlotte's bedroom window on the ground floor was open. Manfred lifted her up, and she managed to clamber into to her room and pull Manfred after her, so he was able to go through to his room upstairs. Charlotte felt embarrassed that she was wearing a skirt and felt it was undignified to climb up in front of him. She tried to tuck her skirt between her legs. They did not kiss goodnight. They learned next morning that the owner lived elsewhere and had gone home after locking up for the night, so it was fortunate that the window was open.

All too soon their time together came to an end, and after a breakfast of rye-bread and butter, it was time for them to part. When they said their emotional goodbyes, Charlotte had a feeling they might not see each other again. She last saw Manfred when she caught the little slow mountain train that took her to Leipzig station where, in contrast to the peace and quiet of the mountains, all was a chaos of refugees, noise, and commotion. Charlotte felt unsafe; she was worried about her safety in a situation where there was no sense of law and order. She said in the confusion of people she was afraid of pickpockets and thieves.

Although not apparent to Charlotte while she was there on that day, Leipzig was heavily armed, and it was about to become the site of Germany's last stand until it surrendered on the 20 April 1945. By this time, Hitler had ordered that members of the Hitler Youth and mostly old men over 65 and even boys aged 16 were to be forced into the Volkssturm or people's army. Some of these had been sent to Leipzig where they would become part of the force following Hitler's orders to defend the city at all costs, even as the Americans approached in April 1945. In the face of the inevitable, the Mayor of Leipzig and his wife committed suicide on 18 April.

At the station at Leipzig, Charlotte searched for a locomotive for her train journey to Hanover, and then she would need one to take her to Hamburg where she would connect with yet another to take her to Vellahn station. Charlotte felt lost and alone and did not know where to go. She looked at the train timetables then enquired from a train driver to get confirmation that his train was going in the right direction for Hanover. It was amazing that trains were still running. She began a long, frightening, and horrendous journey after boarding the train at Leipzig, which passed around Berlin. She found her train was overfull, with people standing or hanging on the luggage racks or clinging outside the train and even on the top of the train in danger of low bridges. Because of the overcrowding, at first Charlotte stood in the aisle and kept checking that her suitcase on the rack above was not being burgled. When some passengers left, she was fortunate enough to get a seat. She could hear the Russian and German artillery whilst on the train. The fighting had moved closer to Berlin during the few days she was with Manfred and was by then getting close to its outskirts. By Saturday, 21 April, Berlin was being shelled, and on 23 April Soviet ground forces entered the outer suburbs of Berlin. By 27 April, Berlin was cut off from the outside world. It was not without good cause on that day that Charlotte became really frightened and afraid for her safety.

The trains and stations by this time were dirty and unkempt, unlike in peacetime. Charlotte had little money, and there were no drinks or food available. On the trains, there was no water or the use of a lavatory since they had not been emptied. Charlotte said the allies were concentrating on destroying the railways and that when there was an air raid warning, the steam train came to a halt, and with the danger of sparks revealing the train, the glowing coals were damped down. The train from Hanover was half in and out of a tunnel when, because the lines ahead en route to Altona, a suburb of Hamburg, had been bombed, all the passengers were told to get off the train. Charlotte set off to make her way on foot, carrying her heavy suitcase to continue her journey. She was directed from there towards a station on the other side of Hamburg where she hoped she could catch a train to Vellahn.

When she got off the Hanover train a young U-boat officer lieutenant spoke to Charlotte. He explained that he had been ordered to go on leave for three days because his submarine was lying damaged at Hamburg. It was most likely at Wilhelmshaven harbour. He said he had nothing to do because his home was too far away in Southern Germany for him to visit his family, and he offered to walk with Charlotte to the next station. She was pleased and grateful to have his company. He carried her suitcase all the way to

Hamburg, where there were signs of the bombing, and accompanied her further as she sought to find her way round Hamburg and outwards to reach another station where she hoped to catch a train to take her to her local station at Vellahn. It was a long walk to get to the other side of Hamburg. Eventually, she saw a train that had come to a halt between stations because it could not get nearer to Hanover, but it was able to take her eastwards to Vellahn. Without a thought, she went into the air raid shelter at Altona station, which is on the outskirts of Hamburg where there was water available and the use of a lavatory. She hurried into the toilet, feeling scared that the train might leave without her, but it didn't, and she caught the train back to Vellahn station and home to the farm at Banzin, leaving the young submarine officer, who would then have had to retrace his steps a distance of some miles.

The officer had been sent away from his U-boat without food, but Charlotte said that soldiers could expect to be given food. Is it possible that he had not realized the war was lost? It is probable that all U-boat offensives would have ended before his boat was back in use because the allies were continually bombing and attacking the U-boat shelters and yards. To this day, Charlotte is very thankful that the young officer who had walked with her for some miles had been trustworthy at a time when there was so much confusion and she was feeling vulnerable and frightened for her life. But she is amazed that they never exchanged names and she so regrets not having had a further opportunity to thank him for his helpful company on a truly frightening day.

She said it was a little romance on a day when she had been so worried and scared for her safety particularly near Hamburg/Berlin where she could hear the artillery. During her journey that day, she had changed trains four times. It is possible that the officer who had accompanied her had gained some comfort from being with Charlotte in their shared experience of fear.

By this time, the Germans were fighting against the world, including the Balkan states, and the Soviet Army, which was moving at great speed towards Berlin, spurred on by Stalin. He had ordered his Soviet Marshals Georgy Zhukov and Ivan Konevto to compete against each other to reach Berlin first. And Charlotte's frightening journey was taking place at this time when Germany was being attacked from all sides. Hamburg was enduring bombing raids between 18 April and 3 May 1945. Charlotte had been in a most dangerous situation. The British assault on the city on 28 April was against an army composed of all kinds of Germans, including the Volkssturm and the Hitler Youth, who were again fighting fiercely in desperation. They put up a strong defence but although there was no hope of winning, they were ordered not to surrender.

When Charlotte reached home at the end of what had turned out to be a perilous and frightening journey after leaving Manfred, she was low in spirits and depressed. Her brother was dead, she was an orphan. She had no family home, and her so special wartime romance had had a dramatic, perilous finish and was ending in extreme sadness. In this frame of mind, she felt her life had stopped. She wrote to Manfred at his home address in Freiburg and told him their friendship could not continue. Unlike fictional romances, Manfred did not write back. Charlotte felt hurt because she was in love and hoped he would have tried to dissuade her from that decision. But she cannot be sure that he had received her letter. She thinks it unlikely he would have received orders to return to the fighting. She has no idea what happened to him from the moment she left him, although she would so very much like to know.

Yalta

Stalin, Roosevelt, and Churchill, had met at the Crimean resort of Yalta, to plan the reorganisation of Germany. It was the second wartime meeting of the Allied leaders. They hoped to define the post-World War II peace and set the stage for rebuilding Europe. The Conference was held between 4 and 11 February 1945, and Germany was to be divided up into four zones. The Yalta Agreement information had filtered through to the population. It was published in newspapers and became common knowledge. The published news was most unwelcome to Charlotte for she discovered from it that Mecklenburg, including Ludwigslust, Banzin, and Schwerin would be in the Russian Zone. This would have a major effect on her future and that of her family.

Good Advice Given?

One day during these last unsettling days of the war, Charlotte set out on her way to the dentist in Parchim. It was the nearest dental practice in Mecklenburg, but it was several train stations away from the farm. In Parchim, completely by chance, she saw her old school friend Edith, who was her best friend from Hanover. Edith told her she was part of a work party, working on the land. Because Edith had stayed at school in Hanover until she was 18, she was doing her Pflicht year later than Charlotte had done and was wearing her brown land workers' uniform. She was based at a camp, from where she was sent out to a farm each day to provide a form of cheap labour. Charlotte had heard through Radio Luxemburg how near the Russians were approaching, and she knew also that the war was lost from listening to the radio. Goebbels, Minister of Propaganda, banned listening to foreign stations, and anyone doing so could have received the death penalty. Though it was forbidden, Charlotte listened to it regularly to learn the progress of the war because she doubted the newspapers' version of events. Under censorship, the message was that the war was going well, although that was patently untrue as contradictory information from the East was filtering through, and it was evident that they were losing the war. Edith was unaware of this news and was going to return to the camp that day as usual, but Charlotte urged her to disobey orders and try to disappear. She told her to take what she could and include something to eat and warm clothes and get away immediately. Charlotte had also learned that the River Elbe was to be the border between the Allies and the Russians. We shall learn more how Edith took Charlotte's advice seriously to leave for Hanover immediately, although it was a good distance away in war-torn Germany. Luckily for Edith, Hanover was destined to be in an Allied zone.

Charlotte was herself in a very unsafe/precarious position, but what could she do? Where could she go to be safe? The Banzin farm was situated on the eastern side of the Elbe so was destined to be in the Soviet Zone, and the Russians were rapidly approaching. The war felt as though it were on her doorstep, and it probably was. Unbeknown to her, there had been a push towards Berlin by the Russian marshals from the east and by the Allies from the west. The Free French Army was approaching from the south.

In accordance with the Yalta agreement, the Americans were to stop when they reached the Elbe and wait until the English and the Russians also arrived at their particular destinations along the River Elbe. The English and the

Americans reached the Elbe in April. Eisenhower had ordered the Americans to stop at the Elbe from 15 April and not proceed to Berlin. The war continued for three more weeks. The Russians approaching from the East were still fighting their way there as the Germans under Hitler's orders not to surrender continued to resist at dreadful cost to all sides.

Charlotte had realized the fragility of her situation when she became aware of the Americans presence close to the farm at Banzin. We have seen that because of the agreement at Yalta, the allies orders were to not cross the River Elbe even though feasible. They were to wait until all the Allies reached their allotted side of the river. The Americans had arrived first at the River Elbe in Mecklenburg and kept their tanks and artillery in place opposite but some distance and out of sight of the farm at Banzin where it seems they were to remain. In spite of the distance, Charlotte described how inexplicably each day at 12 noon the Americans would use their artillery to shoot across the River Elbe towards the farm. And each day before 12, the cows and horses had to be brought out of the stables onto the fields before the Americans began shooting in that direction. After about 20 minutes, the shooting stopped, and the animals were returned to the stables. Charlotte said the guns were pointed in the same direction each time. She thought the Americans could not be bothered to change the position of the artillery, which created some damage to the stables, which had to be mended. It became a daily pattern of behaviour. On the face of it, it seems as lawless as the Wild West.

The stables at Banzin were situated on one side of an open square, and on another side, was the large, stuccoed house, which had the appearance of a little castle and was occupied by the owner and his wife. Sometimes the owner had invited Charlotte for evening drinks but she was not happy about that. She thought he was condescending. On the third side of the square was the working farmhouse where the farmer and his family and Charlotte and a number of POWs and farm workers lived. The whole contained the several different nationalities including Germans, Poles, Yugoslavs, and French and also the Polish officers that were passing through. It all seems surreal. Charlotte said she wasn't afraid. She just accepted and adapted to each new situation.

Hitler's Suicide, 30 April 1945

It can be seen that by this stage in the war all was in turmoil. Everything was falling apart. Hitler could not face reality. He was convinced the war could be won right until the final Soviet assault on the River Oder when the German front caved in. He retreated into his bunker and while the Battle of Berlin raged above he continued issuing orders to attack the Russians and to defend Berlin. Only on 22 April 1945 did Hitler finally accept the war was lost after the setback on 20 April, his 55th birthday, when the Soviet Army shelled Berlin. On 21 April, Soviet troops were at the outer suburbs of Berlin, and on 23 April started to penetrate its outer suburbs. By the 27 April, Berlin was cut off from the outside world.

Meanwhile, in March or April, Hitler had become suspicious of Himmler, who was attempting to negotiate with the Allies. From his bunker near the Reich Chancellery, true to form, Hitler continued to order his generals not to surrender, although the situation was dire. His orders were for them to continue the fight. He seemed to believe that sheer force of will would prevail over obstacles and achieve victory. On 29 April, he married Eva Braun and wrote his last will and testament, naming Karl Dönitz as his successor. On the following day, 30 April 1945, he committed suicide. Hitler died a coward, while still urging others to fight to their death.

When Hitler killed himself on 30 April, Admiral Karl Dönitz became head of state, President of Germany, and Supreme Commander of the armed forces. And although Hitler was dead, the war did not suddenly come to an end. Admiral Dönitz would not order the signing of the German instruments of surrender in Rheims until 7 May 1945. In the meantime, Berlin underwent continuing massive destruction, and the SS shot anyone trying to desert. Many of the people in the cities who were in great danger were innocent people and not Nazis. They included Jews who had somehow managed to hide or be hidden throughout the war and also the forced labourers from other countries, including those from France. In the last week of April, it had become clear that Germany had lost the war. It seems the Russians had battled to take over Berlin between 16 April and 2 May. The Battle for Berlin, on 2 May, has been described by historians as one of the most intense battles in human history. The city was defended by an army, which included the Volkssturm army of old men and young boys of the Hitler Youth, at dreadful cost to all. They had been ordered to continue the fight for the Führer and would fight to the death against the Russians on the front line in Berlin.

On 30 April, the Russians entered Hitler's bunker and searched for him. They eventually discovered the burned bodies of Hitler and Eva Braun, buried in the Chancellery garden. Hitler and Eva had killed themselves on 30 April 1945. In that last week of April, it was clear the war was lost for the Germans.

The Soviet Army continued the bombardment until the city surrendered on 2 May. On this day, the guns stopped firing, and there was a deafening silence. Then began the race to be first to raise the Hammer and Sickle on the Reichstag. By 2 May, the Reichstag had fallen, and the red flag was photographed over the Reichstag. Germany's unconditional surrender followed on 7 May. The document was signed on 8 May, which became known as VE Day ('Victory in Europe Day').

After the battle between 18 April and 3 May, the Americans occupied Nuremburg, and the British occupied Hamburg on 3 May. It seems a decision had been made by Eisenhower to allow the Russians to enter Berlin first. This was agreed partly to save the lives of the other allied soldiers. The Russians suffered enormous casualties, as did the Germans in the fight to take Berlin. Then followed a shocking time of turmoil for the Germans, and it has been recorded that a great degree of ill treatment was perpetrated against women, who were assaulted or worse. Revenge would be exacted by the Soviets on the Germans. It seems that starving and malnourished citizens competed with each other for anything to eat. It has been said that some women found themselves in this new reality stupidly greeting others with 'Heil Hitler'.

Because of his refusal to admit defeat and by ordering the fight to continue, Hitler caused the needless loss of life of hundreds of thousands of extra casualties and the destruction by the allies of more lovely towns and cities in Germany. In the last months of the war, the Nazis were still fighting desperately, killing thousands on the battlefield and in the concentration camps and causing death and terror among citizens. V rockets were launched from mobile starting ramps to damage and terrorize foreign cities.

As the line of contact between Soviet and other Allied forces formed, Tante Lotti's town of Ludwigslust was first captured by British troops, then handed over to the American troops until the Russians arrived to replace one dictatorship with another. Charlotte has described Ludwigslust as a gem of classical architecture with wide cobbled roads, where houses are close to each other and have retained their character. She said it was not bombed, possibly because of its cultural significance, but that stray bombs led to some damage, and she had helped to replace tiles on her uncle and aunt's house on one of her visits. She feels Ludwigslust existed to a large extent in its own time and, compared with so many German towns, was perhaps not much affected by the turmoil around it. But there was more than met the eye.

It was on 2 May 1945, the day of the unconditional surrender, that another example of the Nazis' cruel behaviour was exposed. It was situated not far from Ludwigslust, Charlotte's 'gem of a town'. Close to Ludwigslust with all its beauty, the Americans discovered another example of the Nazis' shameful secrets. The SS had established a camp, a subcamp of Neuengamme concentration camp in February 1945. But the camp had turned into a chamber of horrors when, in April, the SS began using it as a holding camp for some of the mass movement of prisoners from concentration camps outside Germany. More and more emaciated victims were brought or marched there from long distances away, causing unimaginably dreadful overcrowding. Thousands of prisoners were crammed in without food or sanitation, leading to disease, starvation, and death on a large scale. Once again, there would be no compassion shown to these victim until, on the 2 May, the camp was liberated by the soldiers of the US army 82nd Airborne division, but it was much too late for them to save the weakest prisoners.

The US army confronted the citizens of Ludwigslust with what had been going on at Wöbbelin. It seems that, however unlikely that could be, they said it existed without their knowledge. The horrified local inhabitants were ordered to walk through the awful scene and were made to help to bury the dead. Later, they had to attend memorial services and create memorial gardens to the dead in Ludwigslust. Charlotte said, in the town's defence, that the inhabitants, including Onkel Franz and Tante Lotti, and also her great uncle, who lived in Ludwigslust, would not have been aware of it.

Wöbbelin camp was constructed very late in the war. It was in an area not far from where Charlotte was a pupil at her uncle's school and where she had played at being in the Jungmädelbund while living with Tante Lotti. She still finds it beyond comprehension that such a thing could have happened in a place full of her childhood memories.

Escape

By May 1945, Charlotte had been at the farm at Banzin for only about 18 months, although after so many unlikely experiences, it seems longer. It was at that moment that the German Motorized Signal Corps, based at a village near to the farm, was ordered to leave. They had been told the war was lost and they should get away to escape the approaching Russians. They were told they could take civilians with them, but when Charlotte was approached, she told them she would stay at the farm as she wasn't afraid of any Russians. She says she felt untouchable until she was without protection and in about half a day regretted her decision.

The family of the farm's owner, whose wife had been shot at when on a train, had already left. Charlotte quickly decided she would leave, too, although she now feels guilty that she left when asked to stay by the farmer's wife, with whom she had been running the farm after the husband had been forced to join the Volkssturm army. Part of her felt she was letting them down. When the wife of the farmer said she would be staying, Charlotte said, 'the Russians will take over the farm and we have no food for them. We will be helpless so I am leaving.' Charlotte thinks the farmer's wife with her three small children may have chosen to stay so that her husband would be able to find her when he returned from fighting. Charlotte said she felt no affinity with her employers at the farm. We shall learn that that one day it was brought home to her that her decision to leave the farm and Banzin was the right one.

Without saying goodbye, Charlotte turned her back on the farm that day, never again to see any of those, whose lives she had shared, with one exception.

Charlotte spoke to me of items she had stored at Vellahn station in wicker containers especially made for the task for those planning to catch the train. Only later, when collecting her stored items, did she discover an item was missing and she suspects the stationmaster was the culprit. She is vague about when this happened. But it is likely that this was when she gathered items to put in her suitcase to escape from the farm on her bike.

By early 1945, hundreds of thousands of people, including children, were heading westwards in an attempt to surrender to the Western Allies. They were taking heed of Hitler's warning about the Russians' brutality and the fear of what might be done to women. Charlotte went into survival mode. Hurriedly, she also prepared to leave, choosing only things she needed to survive that would fit in the one suitcase that refugees were allowed. The rest of her personal possessions were left at the farm in the cellars that once stored winter food but where belongings had been put when all food was gone. Among the personal things she left were photographs. She now regrets this dearly. There were also two bookshelves, containing books belonging to herself and Jürgen, and some clothes and ornaments. She strapped the suitcase to her bicycle and cycled away from the farm, intent on getting away quickly and perhaps hoping to catch up with the Signal Corps' convoy. She set off along the minor road from the farm to reach the main Hamburg to Berlin road, without actually knowing where her destination should be. But, as she travelled, her intention was to get to the Danish border and from there to neutral Sweden, to her relatives. She was surprised and very relieved to find the Signal corps convoy had made a slow journey and had stopped at Vellahn. When she caught up with the convoy, she unstrapped her leather and wicker suitcase and dumped her bicycle, never to see it again. Often, she finds herself wondering who might have made use of it. It was Anneliese's bicycle that is shown in the photograph of Jürgen, Anneliese, and Charlotte outside Tante Lotti's house. The same bicycle that Charlotte had ridden over cobblestones to collect milk in a churn before being taking it to the farm at Banzin. We wonder if someone was very grateful to find an abandoned bicycle. She feels aggrieved that it had to be abandoned because she had replaced Anneliese's saddle for a larger, adult one. In her memory, she pictures it still standing there.

The greatest benefit to the Swedish population of their being neutral was that they avoided being attacked. That meant that Charlotte expected it to be safe to go to her relatives who were living there.

This episode in Charlotte's journey is quite confusing because she cannot remember clearly how, and in what order, events took place after she caught up with the convoy. She remembers trying to sleep in the telephone exchange building in Vellahn. There she spent the worst night; she had ever experienced by lying on a transformer among metal containers with wires and connecters that hummed noisily and incessantly all night. Next morning, she was allowed to join the convoy of about a dozen vehicles with all its military equipment of the Signal Corps of the Wehrmacht and Waffen SS, which operated military communications. With her suitcase containing her few possessions she became a passenger in a camouflaged army car.

It was not long before the journey became even more frightening. It could be seen clearly that the road ahead was filled with vehicles. Charlotte said that in front and behind her were thousands of refugees, displaced and desperate people. These included families fleeing westwards on foot to escape out of Germany and away from the Russians. She said it had not been possible to pick up information even from rumours in the confusion of desperate people, some of whom were from East Prussia, the Baltic, and Poland.

Those in the convoy could see the flares from the English planes strafing the roads along which people were trying to escape. The flares lit them up as sitting targets. The road became blocked by burning and broken-down vehicles, causing the military convoy to swerve all over the place to try to avoid them. Swerving round obstacles meant they made very slow progress. Charlotte could see that there were fires and flares way ahead, and in all the noise, pandemonium, and mayhem of the aircraft noise, she shouted to the driver of her vehicle that it was too dangerous to stay on that road and that they must turn off to the side at the next opportunity. At first, the military refused to turn off, so she gave them an ultimatum, ordering them at the next turn to stop and give her her luggage. After having a discussion, the soldiers had a change of heart and decided they would turn off after all. They had to head westwards out of Germany towards Denmark without the benefit of road signs, which had been removed because of the war. Charlotte said she had a good sense of direction, which helped at this time. She said that, as far as she knows, the rest of the Signal Corps continued forging ahead, although they could see that the route ahead of them was under attack and in flames. They were continuing to follow orders, although they were sitting targets. That was the mentality, she said, that they followed orders, even though Hitler was mad.

It seems surprising, although it is perhaps a measure of the confusion being experienced at that time, that Charlotte cannot remember hearing the momentous news that Hitler was dead, even though his death had been announced to the German nation on the radio by Admiral Dönitz on 1 May, when it was overheard by Karl Lehmen for the BBC. The Germans would learn that Hitler had committed suicide on 30 April and that he had not died bravely in combat. He had waited a further week, even though he knew on 22 April that the war was lost, which caused the destruction of towns and lives to continue.

Goebbels, whom Hitler in his last will and testament had made Reich Chancellor, had held that position for only one day before he and his wife Magda murdered their children before committing suicide on 1 May, the day after Hitler's death. Charlotte finds it abhorrent that a man could kill his own children.

It was probably only a day of travelling, but it seemed a lot longer. It was possibly in the early hours of 6 May that the vehicle in which Charlotte was travelling entered Schleswig. It had the appearance of a friendly, peaceful German town. It was the last town on the German border with Denmark, but to the escapees' dismay, they found the border was closed, and they were told they could not go through, so they could only turn into side streets. Charlotte was in a place of which she had never heard and was anxious because she was desperate to find somewhere to wash herself as she was experiencing her monthly period. She knocked on a door and told the owner of the house she needed soap and water. The owner was friendly but told her she would have helped but that there wasn't any water as it had been cut off because the war was lost. Charlotte was directed to a labour camp once used by workers in brown uniforms where there were communal bunkrooms for sleeping. She was not allowed to leave the camp. She was just one day too late to be allowed through the border into Denmark and then on to her uncle's family home in Sweden.

Nevertheless, although homeless, she was relieved to be in the English Zone, away from the Russians. But if she had arrived even only one day sooner, the outcome for her life would have been very different, and I would not be writing her story.

The German forces, including those in Denmark and the Netherlands, had surrendered on 4 May 1945. Denmark had become officially free of German control on 5 May when Field Marshall Montgomery had accepted unconditional surrender of Germany's armed forces to CMC 21 Army Group of the large area that included Holland, northwest Germany, Schleswig Holstein, and Denmark. Nazi

Germany had not surrendered until 7 May 1945, and the allies accepted the unconditional surrender on 8 May 1945. In Britain, there was much rejoicing and celebrating of VE Day. Nazi Germany had been defeated.

The War Is Over

Charlotte's hopes of reaching her relatives in Sweden were thwarted. All refugees had to be checked to make sure no Nazis got through. The authorities wished to de-Nazify them.

In Schleswig, Charlotte stayed with the military at first where, as one of the displaced, she was given food. There was a field kitchen in the English Zone, a big pot of food, which had been part of the German military occupation and had been kept on the go.

Schleswig was under the jurisdiction of the Allies in May 1945. Though the camp was in the English Zone, volunteers ran it. There was no government. But at least there was food again. Charlotte spoke of there being so much meat to eat because cattle had been slaughtered once there was no longer anything left in the fields for fodder in the flat farming country. This had created a glut of certain types of food, then nothing.

She said, while she was in the refugee camp for a week, she was looked after and meals were provided. She sunbathed and relaxed on the shore of the Baltic Sea. It was lovely weather, and with no decisions to be made, it seemed more like a holiday. But she was a stateless refugee whose future was very much in doubt. She felt for quite a while that her life was on halt.

She felt a sense of relief that the war was over although Germany had been defeated. Hitler was dead, and gone was his power over the life and death of millions. Charlotte felt let down by him. She feels bitter that her lovely brother died because of him.

The English wanted to dissolve the camp where she was, so they arranged transport to move people out. Charlotte was offered transport and given a choice of where she wished to be repatriated. She chose Hanover, where she had friends, and was driven there in an English army truck. When they were about to be dispersed, the refugees were given a big lump of lard, wrapped in paper, to take with them. These were from the enormous storerooms that had been kept by the German military.

An Allied advance ground force had reached Hanover in April 1945. In early May, with only her few possessions, Charlotte was dropped off by the English to find her own way on a main road on the outskirts of the poor side of Hanover, in an area that was unknown to her. Her immediate concern was to find somewhere to live. She had chosen to go to Hanover because she was hoping she would find someone she knew, but she had no idea who had survived or whose homes had been destroyed during the many bombing raids. She was alone with nowhere to go. She was shocked by the sight of the destruction in the city that had borne the brunt of the repetitive bombing, which had destroyed much of the city centre and half of all the buildings. Mounds and mounds of rubble had been created. After making enquiries, including from a tram driver, about how to get to Hanover Süd, where she had friends, she was advised to go first to the authorities to register as a refugee and then on to the housing department. Although the English were in overall control in Hanover, the Germans had been kept in their jobs by the English and were allocating addresses to homeless refugees. They were directing them to possible places where they could stay.

The suggested accommodation was in the homes of people who had had to relinquish part of their living space. Charlotte and another girl refugee whom she had met set off to search for the address on the paper given them but found the paper was out of date. Some addresses being offered no longer existed, including their allocated room in someone's home. The girl had led Charlotte to believe she was going to be her companion, but she had not told her the truth and had been in touch with her boyfriend. She left with him, and he took her somewhere else to live, leaving Charlotte on her own. Charlotte felt betrayed because she thought she was looking after the girl. Because the allocated room had been filled already, the owner of the room allocated suggested she enquire at an upstairs flat. Charlotte used her thumb to hide the out-of-date number on the piece of paper when she enquired at the room on a higher floor. She was offered a room that had only a hard couch or the hard floor on which to sleep. The room was uncomfortable and in a horribly poor area on the outskirts of Hanover, and she stayed for only one night.

She also describes staying in a house where two girls slept in one room and Charlotte was in another with a young man where she had to sleep on a table. As it happens, the flat had been in Hanover Linden. Hanover Linden was the poor area of Hanover, where her father had taken her as a child to see the masses of communist flags hung in the streets and where she had felt out of place and nervous. Hitler had made sure that neither the communists nor their flags still remained.

The next day, Charlotte set out on public transport to the inner city to find the home of her friend Merigart, to whose home she had run away when she was aged 13. Merigart and her family were pleased to see her, but their home, a flat with four floors had, like so many others, been bombed. Only half of the block remained. The back wall of the whole of the block of flats had been blown off. Charlotte was able to sleep in a room at the back, although it was open to the elements. She remembers a pretty screen, which was provided to shield her so that she could get washed and dressed without being seen. Luckily, it was nice summer weather during June 1945. It could only be a temporary stay as the house was damaged. Charlotte felt it was not safe and that the house could collapse. Other residents of Hanover remained in their badly damaged houses by moving into the cellars where they survived. Perhaps, like Tante Lotti's cellar in Ludwigslust, the houses would have had storerooms for apples and potatoes and another for fruit and preserves, which, in peacetime, were stored on shelves in 'Kilner' jars. Vitally, the cellars could provide water if they also contained a laundry area, perhaps like Tante Lotti's, where there was a huge copper with a fire beneath for washing the sheets, and a coal cellar.

Charlotte had taken with her to her friend's house the 5-lb portion of lard given to her when she was dropped off in Hanover by the English. Charlotte finds it hard to recollect what happened to the lard but is sure the family would be delighted with it because they would not have seen any for so long. In peacetime, the lard would have been turned into something special with extra ingredients such as apples or whatever else was available. Nevertheless, it would have been a welcome treat.

With the surrender of the Germans, the money in German bank accounts was immediately worthless. No one was rich unless they had land, gold, jewellery, or silver. Although it had become valueless, Charlotte kept her father's pre-war bank book.

A New Way of Life, May 1945

Charlotte's next urgent need, when she was aged about 18 or 19, was to find work. She needed money to be able to pay rent for any accommodation, so she went to the English headquarters to ask for work. The English ruled from the former German premises. When asked what she could do, she said she had secretarial qualifications and she could boil. She actually meant she could cook so this was thought funny. Fortunately, she had learned English at school and she was offered work in the sergeants' mess. Here, she would meet blond-haired Michael Fellows, who was to play an important part in her life. At the sergeants' mess, Frau Riemann, a solicitor's wife, was in charge. She was herself a refugee. Her husband, Herr Riemann, was a prisoner in Siberia. There was a surplus of help at the sergeants' mess and not really any need to employ Charlotte as an assistant.

Charlotte was desperate to find somewhere to live because the home of Merigart's family was not suitable because it was damaged and brimming full. The solution she chose seems so unlikely, but she says she had little choice. Charlotte went to stay at the home of Erna, her hated stepmother, and Erna's son Klaus. For Erna, it was better to have Charlotte to stay with her, otherwise she would have had to have someone she did not know. Charlotte's father and Erna had moved out of the family home in Hanover into the smaller flat at Nisburg, a suburb of Hanover, before Andreas went into the Paradise home for those with dementia. Because the new flat was small, many family possessions had been left behind, but some had been kept, including some of the items inherited from Charlotte's mother Muschi and from the rest of the family. These included family portraits, including the one of Theodor Martin Krabbe.

Figure 32 Charlotte and stepbrother Klaus

When he was about seven years old, Charlotte's stepbrother Klaus used to visit her at the sergeants' mess on his way home from school. For a few weeks, he caught a later bus home so he could visit. Charlotte liked seeing him. He was given food at the mess, and even if Charlotte was not there, he was still given treats.

Figure 33 Michael in Royal Engineers uniform

After a few days working in the sergeants' mess at Hanover, Charlotte met Michael Fellows, a Sapper in the Royal Engineers in 29th Field Squadron in the army of occupation. She learned that he had taken part in the D-Day landings on 6 June 1944, which were part of Operation Overlord during the attempt to enter Europe, which was defended like a fortress.

Michael would describe his experience of that day in the following article written for *Saga Magazine* on the fiftieth anniversary of the landings:

MICHAEL FELLOWS
20, Sapper, Royal Engineers
'We were lowered from troopships at about 4am into fast, small boats – about 14 seasick sappers crammed

into each boat. We landed before the tanks with 25lb of high explosive on each hip to blow up the anti-tank obstacles strung along the beach.

We did this constantly, apart from some night hours spent in a small slip trench I had dug in the sand. I threw away my rifle because I couldn't run properly with the weight of the explosives. At dawn we moved inland and started clearing anti-tank and anti-personnel mines in the fields and along the verges of the narrow Normandy lanes. By now the beach was littered with knocked-out vehicles and bodies – mainly infantry which had been coming in all day under heavy fire from mortars, heavy artillery and, further inland, machine-guns in pillboxes (until they were knocked out from the air). I was terrified. The worst day of my life.'

Twelve thousand Allied warships had aimed for the five beaches named Utah, Omaha, Gold, Juno, and Sword to which Michael's unit was allocated. By the end of that day, Allied forces composed of soldiers from so many countries besides those landing from England, America, and Canada, had achieved their aim and amazingly were in Normandy.

Michael told Charlotte that, prior to the landings, his unit had been stationed in Brancaster in Norfolk, East Anglia, during the lead-up to D-Day, where the sweeping sandy beaches resembled those of the Normandy coast and where landings were practised by the American troops. At that time, a false impression was being created to trick Hitler and the Nazis into thinking the attack was to be along the shorter route to Calais. The lengths to which they went make fascinating reading. These included the making of dummy tanks. At 3:00 a.m. on 6 June 1944, Michael's unit was among the first away from Norfolk heading for Normandy to clear the way for the tanks.

In Normandy, Michael and the other engineers, had to deal with the destruction wreaked by the Allied troops as they forged their way towards Germany as well as that created by the defending and retreating Germans in their attempt to thwart the progress of the Allies. The Sappers' work was to clear the way for the Allies. They had to facilitate the replacement and repairing of bridges and any infrastructure destroyed by the retreating Germans. They worked in danger from German artillery fire and crossfire of their compatriots' 'friendly fire'.

Liberators

Charlotte learned that, for a while, the Engineers doing this work were using liberated Paris as a base and were allocated to French families for hospitality. Michael was allocated to a Parisian family who were living in their summer residence at Vernon on the River Seine during the time he was being ordered out to various destinations. Here, he had a romance with the daughter of the family. But by the summer of 1945, Michael was in Hanover, where the Sappers were to help in the rebuilding of the hugely damaged city.

Figure 34 Michael, studio portrait

Michael was based with the troops in accommodation opposite the sergeants' mess. It appears that, probably from the first moment he saw Charlotte at the sergeants' mess in Hanover, Michael fell in love with Charlotte. She was teased because he kept calling to see her, but he persisted. Someone said to Charlotte that they could see that Michael was falling in love with her. The soldiers were not meant to fraternize, but although there was a prohibition on mixing with the Germans, Michael managed to take Charlotte to concerts. He explained how he had made her an imitation Swedish badge on white cardboard, and in spite of its being a crude imitation of a badge, it seems it looked convincing and was effective. She was his girlfriend, and the cardboard badge, although nonsense, was accepted to gain her entrance to concerts of high-class music played by German musicians. On one occasion, in the beautiful Herrenhausen Gardens, which were connected with the English Royal House of Hanover, and on another, to listen by the Maschsee, the lake about which we learned earlier. In those days, she said, once again, everything seemed unreal. The Herrenhausen house had been badly bombed by the Allies. Charlotte said it felt as though it were peacetime. The audience was composed of both English and Germans. But Charlotte describes how the English were privileged and were given good food and entertainment, which was unavailable to others. She remembers experiencing a delicious cream tea. Charlotte and Michael discovered they had similar ideas of life. Both were rebels and of the same mindset.

At the time when she was working in the sergeants' mess, Charlotte needed to find accommodation. Here, she met an elegant stranger named Mignon Lange. When Mignon heard that Charlotte was searching for accommodation, she invited her to stay at her home. Charlotte was grateful and happy to share a twin-bedded bedroom. Mignon had no children, and her husband was another of the Russian prisoners in Siberia. Like Erna, Mignon would also have had someone allocated to share her home if she had not made her own choice. In peacetime, she and her husband had an amateur radio shop in the centre of Hanover, which, amazingly, managed to trade all through the war while he was away and seemingly, miraculously, remained unscathed throughout the bombing. In their home, there was specialized high-quality radio equipment, which allowed her to listen to pirate radio.

Charlotte was able to take home leftover food from the sergeants' mess to share with Mignon. Mignon so appreciated the contribution that she expressed her thanks for several years by sending Charlotte Christmas gifts of special 'Sprengel' chocolates until Charlotte said it shouldn't continue. The chocolates were ordered direct from the makers. Charlotte and Michael, who was now very much part of her life, had other reasons to be grateful to Mignon. To allow them to have time to themselves, Mignon would go to bed early so that Michael and Charlotte could have the sitting room to themselves to have some quiet time alone.

Charlotte said there were no German rulers left after the war. The English had the overall authority to govern Hanover. She said she thought they did it well. They employed Germans in their previous administrative jobs so things went smoothly. But during the occupation, the English could claim someone's home, and Mignon Lange was ordered to move out of her home and look for somewhere else to live. Michael, with an army friend and Herr Lange's friend, plus Charlotte's cousin Gebhard, who had escaped from the East, helped rescue Mignon's possessions. These included specialized sound equipment and furniture, which they put in a safe place. The police station was in a rented house with a cellar beneath. The owner allowed the storage of Mignon's belongings. She had had to make way for the English families of a commissioner, who were moving into her flat. Two soldiers oversaw the move, making sure that stipulated pieces of furniture, including a table and a bed, were left for the new arrivals. Charlotte told me how she chatted to the soldiers to distract them. This enabled more items to be saved than should have been, including luxury Indian carpets, which became included among the items stored in the cellar beneath the police station.

Because Hanover was in the English Zone, Charlotte was able to visit Mignon after the war. She used to go out with her for afternoon tea when visiting friends in Hanover and met Mignon's husband, who had returned from Siberia. He was very pale and thin and seemed damaged by his wartime experiences as a soldier and prisoner of war. He was fortunate to have survived. She said he seemed more of a scientific person and not the kind of person who would choose to be a soldier.

When Mignon's home was requisitioned, Charlotte was left without a home again. Michael managed to find an empty house and helped move her into a semi basement. Essentially, it was a squat. The basement had a window, a washbasin, and lavatory. Two soldiers were residing above, guarding the contents of that house. Looking back on the incident, Charlotte realized she was in a very unsafe position. She was nervous and at night and used to prop a chair under the door handle to keep it secure. The soldiers on one occasion invited her for a cup of tea but did not have friendly intentions. They had put salt in her tea, making it horrible, but she did not complain because she felt vulnerable as she was squatting illegally.

Figure 35 Charlotte (right) and Frau Albert at the officers' mess

Figure 36 Charlotte, aged 20, with 'Madame de Pompadour' hairstyle

The Officers' Mess

To make herself look more grownup, Charlotte changed her hairstyle. Her hair was swept high with combs, and she called it her 'Madame de Pompadour' style. She had contacted the officers' mess and asked if she could have a job, but nevertheless it took her by surprise when she had a call from headquarters, asking her to run the officers' mess. Importantly, the job provided her with accommodation. It entailed working in three houses for twelve officers. The houses were homes that had been requisitioned without warning from the Germans by the English. The English took over large, prosperous houses in the best districts of Hanover. Charlotte lived in an attic in the house with Frau Albert, the wife of one of the German owners, and their daughter Brigitte. The husband and son had to sleep elsewhere and officially were not allowed into the women's rooms but disobeyed that rule when visiting at weekends. One of the houses was designated as the officers' mess and was like a restaurant. The officers had a batman and a servant from the ranks. The other two houses provided living accommodation. Charlotte had a room to herself.

Charlotte was asked to start work at once and even to engage her own German staff, but she became immediately suspicious that someone had been stealing. She discovered unwrapped sausages in two German women's coat pockets because they had not been hidden. They could be seen in the pockets of their see-through overalls. She then confronted the women, who were older than she was, by pointing at the pockets. She said they were shameless. Charlotte did remark that they probably had starving families at home, but she thought it was wrong to steal. She ordered them to take their coats and go straight out, which left her in need of a cook and assistant cook. She had sacked both of them and is amazed she did that at the young age of 20 but had left herself with a problem. By good fortune, Charlotte was delighted and relieved when, fortuitously or miraculously, her best friend Barbara from her days at her uncle's school at Ludwigslust turned up at just the right time. She had somehow got through the border from the Soviet Zone, possibly by using bribery. Barbara took over the duties of both of the sacked women, who had been the cook and assistant cook, and turned out to be a good cook herself and more than capable of doing both tasks. While Barbara became the cook, Charlotte ran the main house.

She spoke of the soldiers receiving what were called comfort boxes, which included cigarettes and soap. She said Michael was nicknamed 'Mouse' because of his liking for cheese. He would exchange his ration of tinned ham for cheese. The Americans sent large composition boxes of iron rations to the mess. They always included a tin of cigarettes and tinned food such as Spam. Charlotte took any spare tins and cigarettes to the market, where she would use them to barter with farmers for fresh vegetables and fruit, including asparagus and strawberries, to create a healthier diet.

As far as Charlotte knows, Barbara's father, who had been so badly wounded in the First World War, was not treated badly by any of the incomers, who in turn were the Americans, the English, and finally the Russians when Ludwigslust became part of the Soviet Union under Stalin.

Frau Albert and family would be Charlotte's friends for the rest of her life except for her son, who tragically committed suicide. Charlotte heard that the daughter of Tante Lotti's neighbour in the Russian Zone had also committed suicide. Some found it difficult to adjust to the reality of life after the war. But more happily for the Albert family, their daughter Brigitte married an English officer and moved with him to a large Regency house in Cheltenham, England. Charlotte and Brigitte took holiday breaks together. They went on spa holidays and, on at least one occasion, booked in for an extra week because they had found it so enjoyable. Charlotte said it was good to feel emancipated, living with their children, enjoying a very different life from that which was traditionally experienced by German housewives.

When Michael was on a course, which he had been offered by the University of Göttingen in Lower Saxony, he used to travel back to Hanover to visit her, although it was difficult travelling through the snow in the severe winter. Somehow, he managed to get to her, although roads were closed. Because there was no transport, he used to thumb lifts, which, Charlotte said, were easy for the English to get. The course was an officer-training course, but Sapper Fellows was a rebel, and he was thrown off the course because he did not follow the rules. Charlotte said at times she felt embarrassed when he ignored rules. He liked to make his own decisions. He would not wear a hat and did not salute officers, but somehow, he often got away with it. However, he was not popular with the major in the regiment because he was not an obedient soldier and was not in favour of marching and parading. Charlotte thinks he was, by this time, beginning to have pacifist leanings.

Michael's Birthday, 1 November 1923, was almost the same as that of Charlotte's brother, who was born on 8 October 1923. Jürgen would have been a month older than Michael if he had not been killed in the East only a few months earlier on 10 July 1944.

On the Buffers

On one occasion, Charlotte and Michael had arranged to meet her mother's brothers' uncles, Oscar and Hans-Hugo Dabelstein, and Hugo's English wife Elsie, at a resort on the River Elbe, at the port of Hamburg. One day, they set out on a train journey from Hanover to visit them in Hamburg. In spite of the bombing that had been aimed at the railway networks, the lines were intact because immediately after any attacks, they had been mended. But the journey turned into an unpleasant ordeal for Charlotte and Michael. The railways and trains, which were once so efficient and reliable, were now old, dirty, and overcrowded. People had no other means of transport because of the lack of petrol, so the train carriages were overflowing with passengers, some of them sitting in the aisles, others clinging at great risk on the sides of the train, without an inch to spare between them, and some on the top of the train, with the added risk posed by narrow and low tunnels or bridges. Because there was no room on the train, Charlotte assures me that it was a joint decision, which she and Michael made, to choose an option that they hoped was less risky. They chose to travel on the train's buffers. There was a little standing space where the buffers met but it was less tiring for Charlotte and Michael to sit down. They quickly bitterly regretted their choice of travel as they endured smoke and grit blowing in their face and eyes all the way from Hanover to Hamburg, a two-hour journey with no stopping points on the way. They had soon discovered it was terribly dangerous and wished they had not chosen that option. Although they arrived at their destination, covered in soot and with sore eyes, they managed to meet up with the relatives and have a pleasant time.

Charlotte told me that the following visit was experienced on the day of that journey on the buffers, but it seems that the first occurrence of this event at Hamburg did not take place until 1952.

It is still a tourist attraction today. Charlotte certainly experienced this sometime when she met a family member in a very pleasant restaurant for afternoon tea where they watched steamers going past. According to a traditional custom, started in 1952, ships above a certain size on their way to Hamburg through a narrow channel on the River Elbe, where it flows out into the North Sea, are greeted in a particular way. The national language of the ship is played over a microphone with their national music booming across the river. Similarly, they are given a traditional farewell on the way back.

One possible tea room was the Blankenese in an expensive part of Hamburg. It had nice cream cakes with lots of whipped cream.

Charlotte's impression was that Hans-Hugo immediately after the war did his best to dissociate himself from his role as an officer in the Nazi army and kept a low profile. She feels he might have been frightened that there might be someone whom he would not wish to recognize him. She has already described his arrogant behaviour, so he may have had just cause to be wary.

Onkel Oscar was a well-off bachelor, who had made his money in jewellery and was known for being generous to members of the family. Onkel Hugo's first wife Erna was German, but when she died, he married Elsie, an English lady, who had been married to an English sea captain, who had died. Charlotte said Elsie had travelled with her husband on his voyages when he was a captain and was allowed to take her own piano on board. When both of the Hanover homes of the uncles and aunt had been bombed, they had to move to rent a flat in Mittelweg.

Figure 37 Charlotte by fountain, Wolfenbüttel, 1945

Wolfenbüttel, 1945 or 1946

Another change occurred for Charlotte when Michael arranged to move her to Wolfenbüttel in 1945 to be with him when his whole unit was moved from Hanover to Wolfenbüttel. It was where the headquarters of his unit was situated. True to form, without asking for permission, Michael borrowed Captain Baldung's car to fetch Charlotte and her belongings. The captain was very annoyed when he discovered that his car was missing, especially so as he had to use his son's bicycle and even more so when, on his bicycle, he recognized Michael and Charlotte as they passed him in his car, which they had had for a whole day. Michael evidently stayed cool and did not stop, which seemed astonishing to Charlotte. This was another example of Michael's disregard for authority. It also showed that the captain approved of Michael because there seem not to have been any unfortunate consequences.

During the time that Charlotte was living in Wolfenbüttel, a wall in Berlin and a border were constructed by the Russians to separate the increasingly oppressive Soviet regime in the East from Western Europe. Winston Churchill would name it the Iron Curtain. Hamburg was in the West at a point where some could gain permission or use bribery to cross into the Soviet Zone. Charlotte's cousin had supposedly set up a possible meeting between her aunts Lotti and Leni and herself at the border to stay for an hour. Somehow, Charlotte and her aunts had been led to believe they could communicate if they met each other on opposite sides of the border closer to Hamburg. They hoped to wave and perhaps call to each other. Tante Lotti had a new suit made especially for the occasion. Mistakenly, they thought they would have one hour, but they had not realized there would be a distance of nearly a kilometre between them. They had such high hopes of seeing each other, but these were dashed because they found themselves too far apart even to see each other, let alone shout or wave to each other across the buffer zone. They were just too far apart. They might as well have been a world apart. That day, they all left dissatisfied and unhappy and so disappointed. In spite of the extreme sense of disappointment and unhappiness, there was one good outcome from the attempted meeting. When Tante Lotti and Tante Leni met each other socially on the Soviet side of the border that day, they discovered they got on and enjoyed each other's company, thus overcoming Tante Lotti's former antipathy towards the Krabbe family.

This had possibly made the long distances they each had made to get to the border a little more worthwhile.

When reflecting on this doomed attempt today, Charlotte finds it difficult to understand how they could all have possibly expected it to be successful.

Great towers had loomed over them that day, manned by armed guards, ready to shoot anyone attempting to cross to the West. Minefields also lay in the way of would-be escapees. The Russians did not want infiltrators or escapees. Charlotte said that among the reasons East Germans wished to escape to the West when they were under the Soviet regime, was that under communism there was free further education, and the universities, where they had to learn the Russian language, were good. Even the not so clever students had the opportunity of obtaining a free university education, but this led to their wanting greater opportunities and freedom. In their attempts to get to the West, they ran the risk of being shot. One of Charlotte's cousins, she said, did manage to get through, but for some mysterious reason, returned into the Soviet Zone before managing to get back again to the West. Charlotte is curious about his motives. People depended on guides, to whom they paid a lot of money, to escape at night.

Besides the disappointment of not being able to see her aunts, Charlotte had another problem because she was living in Hanover in West Germany and not of the legal age of 21 to sign for herself. Her aunts who were her guardians and could have signed legal documents for her, were in Mecklenburg, in a different zone at that time so could not do so. At that time, the postal service was disrupted, too. Because Charlotte was on her own and had not reached the legal age of 21, she applied at the registry office to get the required permission for her to sign legal documents for herself. There she was declared of age to do so and was then able to apply for a passport to visit Sweden.

At Wolfenbüttel, Charlotte became secretary to the major. Neither she nor Michael had much to do while they were there. The job had been created for her, and she received a salary. While there, she used the opportunity to learn Swedish and improve her English from teachers. On one occasion, a domestic helper brought in a stray earing, which she had found in the major's bedroom, to ask what should be done with it. She was told to put it back where it had been found.

Rule-Breaking Trysts

At first, at Wolfenbüttel, Charlotte had accommodation in a private home. It was a bed-sitting room. The situation was unsatisfactory because there was a restriction that meant that Michael was not allowed to visit her. Charlotte said they were naughty and broke the rules. On one occasion, the owner knocked on the door of Charlotte's room while Michael was with her, and she quickly made him hide in the wardrobe. Luckily for them, the owner decided she was alone after he had peered around the room.

But once again, luck was on Charlotte's side when she happened to meet a family at Wolfenbüttel who had a smallholding and because they had killed a pig, they invited her to eat with them. They were a very nice family. They rented her a room, and she was provided with food and heating, and while there, she was able to see Michael freely.

Figure 38 Onkel Herbert Dabelstein

We have seen that Charlotte's attempt to get to her wealthy uncle, Herbert Dabelstein, the brother of her late mother, had been thwarted. When she arrived at Schleswig, she found that Denmark's border was closed because the war had ended, and her plans were changed. Her Onkel Herbert lived at Ängby in Sweden, just outside Stockholm, where he had made a success of the family business after moving from Germany. He wanted Charlotte to stay with him in Sweden. Over the years, he had regularly sent food parcels to his sister Muschi's family in Hanover, which were packed by the Red Cross. Charlotte remembers that she and Jürgen had their own butter dishes, but the disliked housekeeper did not want to accept the parcels because she thought it un-German to accept them. Onkel Herbert also sent the children money for their birthdays.

Charlotte had been unsuccessful with her application to leave Germany while she was a stateless person, so Michael wrote to Ernest Bevin, the Foreign Secretary in Britain's postwar Labour Government, to apply for her to leave Germany. Michael had explained that Charlotte had been only a child at the beginning of the war, so was unlikely to be a Nazi. When he didn't get a reply, he wrote again, and amazingly, her release came through quickly. His persistent nature paid off. The reason why they had difficulty in getting permission to get married in England was because some people pretended they were going to marry just in order to get access to England. She said her move to Sweden was a step nearer to getting out of Germany. Charlotte said later applicants had to pass exams.

Sweden, c. 1946, Aged 19/20

Sweden, which was neutral during the war, seemingly assisted both the German and the Allied cause. For example, it supplied the Nazis with iron ore, which was vital for the production of weapons, but it also supplied the Allies with military intelligence and aided the rescue of Jews. Nevertheless, Sweden avoided being invaded, and unlike German money, which was worthless, Swedish money was not. Charlotte was now free to start her journey to her uncle's home in Sweden. She and Michael found they were sorry that she was now free to leave, and they were unhappy to be parted. The major at Wolfenbüttel, was sympathetic to their feelings and said he would not expect Michael back for three days while he travelled with Charlotte on refugee transport to the Danish border at Schleswig. From Schleswig, the women and children refugees were taken by rail to quarantine at Landskrona in Sweden for two weeks, where they were checked for illnesses. Samples were taken until they were pronounced healthy. Charlotte was then allowed to continue her journey alone by train to Ängby (meaning 'meadow village') near Stockholm in Sweden to stay with her uncle. Herbert Dabelstein was the brother of her deceased mother 'Muschi', Tante Lotti, and uncles Hugo and Oscar.

Her Onkel Herbert had three boys and two daughters and also fostered two girls, who had been starving refugees during Finland's war against Russia. He adopted one as a ward. Onkel Oscar seems to have been a very caring person. After Charlotte had left, Michael remained at Wolfenbüttel, to wait until he was free to return to England and get demobilized in 1947. Charlotte and Michael had never discussed marriage, but it became a foregone conclusion. Their love grew gradually, and they wanted to stay together.

When Charlotte's uncle learned that she wanted to marry Michael, he said he wanted to meet him. Michael could not see any reason why the uncle should want to see him, and his own family was rather upset in 1947 that their only son wanted to use his six weeks' demob leave to go to Charlotte. Michael travelled to Sweden on SS Saga to spend his six weeks demobilization leave at the luxurious home of Charlotte's uncle, where Charlotte and Michael breakfasted each day with him. They felt obliged to stay but made the most of it by using public transport to explore the area by walking and sight-seeing. Michael and her uncle got on well with each other. Charlotte's uncle liked having conversations with Michael and they spoke to each other by using French with the help of a little German. Charlotte was able to converse in both English, which she had learned at school, and Swedish, which, together with English, she had learned from the teachers she met at Wolfenbüttel.

Although her uncle had thought she would stay, Charlotte had not seen a future for herself in Sweden because she was unable to acquire a work permit to work there. She described herself as having an inquisitive disposition and would have been bored without work.

Charlotte was fortunate to have money to spend because she had the money that had been sent by Onkel Herbert to Jürgen and herself every year for their birthdays and Christmas, which they had saved. Combined with Jürgen's share, she had 38 years' worth of accumulated Swedish kronor. She was able to spend this money in Sweden on her trousseau, ordering many items that were later posted to England. These included an eiderdown, bed linen, and a whole dinner service. Her aunt had also made a button-through dress for her from white linen sheets that she had stored. It had epaulettes and was pleated. It was usual for a dressmaker to come to the home to do garment alterations and to make clothes. Charlotte remembers standing on a table for the dress to be pinned and that the pins of so many pleats scratched her legs when she moved whilst being fitted. The buttons for the dress were made of real mother-of-pearl, taken from a dress shirt of her grandfather Dabelstein.

A New Start

Charlotte left Sweden to join Michael in England during the summer of 1947 and travelled on the SS Saga, the same ship on which Michael had travelled to visit her. The ship docked at Dover on 1 August, which was a Bank holiday. She had expected the victor of the war to be rich, so was shocked, while travelling on overcrowded and dirty trains, to see the effects that the war had had on England. She was surprised to see that much of Birmingham had suffered from bombing raids. She would not have known the Old Market Hall in the Bull Ring in Birmingham before it was left with only its walls standing after an incendiary fire in August 1940. The Bull Ring Centre has since been rebuilt at least twice since the war's end. Then Charlotte took the taxi journey to Michael at his parents' home in Sandwell road, Handsworth, which revealed a pleasant suburb, untouched by bombing. The detached Edwardian House was on a wide treelined main road, with a strip of grass along its length, which was once intended for a tramway but never developed.

Figure 39 Charlotte and Michael, Wedding Day, 1947

On 9 August 1947, a week after arriving in England, Charlotte who was just aged 21, was married to Michael by special licence from the Archbishop of Canterbury at St James Church in Sandwell, Birmingham. There was a small wedding party of six. Charlotte, who had a slim waist, wore a cream two-piece shantung silk wedding dress, which had been given to her by her aunt when she was in Sweden. The aunt had given her some other nice clothes, too. Clothes were rationed in England, but she managed to buy some smart, light-beige-coloured shoes. The price of her shoes was written in chalk on the sole of her shoes, which, she later realized, would have been seen when she was kneeling in church. Michael was wearing his demob suit. Its sleeves were too long, and his shoes far too large for his small feet, leaving a gap at the sides. There was no alternative, though, and they looked funny. Following the ceremony, they enjoyed a hot meal at the New Inn Public House in Handsworth Wood. Built in 1901, it is now a Grade-II listed building, called the New Inns Public House.

Figure 40 Michael's parents

Michael's parents were welcoming. At first, they had thought that Charlotte was Swedish but happily accepted her when they knew she was German. Charlotte remembers them with great fondness. She said they were very nice and used to stay with them at their home in Hemingford Abbots.

Adapting to Life in England

Charlotte and Michael had one week's honeymoon at a hotel just outside Birmingham. To get access to country walks, they caught a tram as far as the bus terminus on the Birmingham outskirts, and they walked in the Clent Hills of Worcestershire. On one occasion, they walked as far as Bromsgrove and then had to hurry to catch the last tram of the day, which would leave the terminus at 10.00 p.m. On another occasion, they visited the well-known beauty spot of the Lickey Hills, just outside of Birmingham. Today, it is a country park, with a visitor centre. Michael introduced Charlotte to cricket, and they watched matches in the local park. Charlotte thought the English were mad to play such a game. They lived for a while at Michael's parents' house, where they had a bedroom and a sitting room to themselves. Michael's mother was welcoming and thought, by providing Charlotte with a cup of 'Camp coffee', real coffee probably not being available, that she was doing something special for Charlotte. Charlotte thought it an unpleasant drink and said she would prefer tea.

Michael had returned to his job at Wakeman's Property and Construction Consultants in Edgbaston, Birmingham, where he had been articled as a quantity surveyor when he left Aston Grammar school, aged 16, in 1939. During the time before he went to Brancaster, he had to build an underground factory at the motor works, at Longbridge in Birmingham. Michael said he hated it. While working on the tunnels, he had had his arm broken by a runaway truck. There were no health and safety rules then. The tunnels were hidden to protect thousands of, mainly women, munitions workers from German bombers. Munitions workers produced the Merlin engines for Spitfires and Hawker Hurricanes. The tunnels were also to provide shelter from air raids. Michael was exempt from the war until he was called up for D-Day because of low numbers.

Michael was only accepted back at Wakeman's Consultants firm because he had returned from the war, although there was not enough work for him. Charlotte found work for herself as a clerk at £5.00 per week but left after six months. She took another job, working for two men, who paid her for doing nothing in one room with a funny smell. She left again for a distribution firm along the Bristol Road, where she worked until 1948. She remembers walking home in the dreadful smog, which was caused by pollution. It was so thick she could not see her way home in 1947. Charlotte said her six months of living in the Handsworth area were pleasant, although she was shocked to see that the Birmingham slum areas were worse than the poor communist area she had visited in Hanover Linden. Michael was not made welcome at his former firm because there was not a vacancy for him. His pay at £5 per week was no more than Charlotte was getting in her temporary workplaces.

Charlotte was horrified by the unhygienic conditions in food shops in Birmingham, where raw meats and cured meats were displayed in close proximity and were breathed over by customers queuing for their rationed allowance. Food had been sold more hygienically in glass cases in Germany. The Marshall Plan in 1948 aided Germany's recovery. Charlotte described it as a bulwark.

My first thought was that, after such a varied, unpredictable, and often odd way of life whilst she was growing up in Germany, her new life in England must have been an anti-climax for Charlotte, but she said that it did not seem that way. Her first challenge was that of conversing in a language that was not her own.

Tante Lotti and Tante Leni in the Soviet Zone

Meanwhile, Tante Lotti and Tante Leni were also experiencing a huge change to their lives after the surrender of the Germans. Charlotte thinks that information about their change of circumstances filtered through from the family. She used the word 'rumours' for the details she picked up. Because Charlotte's relatives were living in the Soviet Zone, she was unable to visit them, but Tante Lotti eventually wrote to her from Ludwigslust to tell her what was happening in her life. There was censorship, but her aunt did not attempt to hide her feelings of contempt for the Russians and cursed them. However, her letters still managed to get through.

Charlotte learned that at first the Americans had occupied all of Mecklenburg because they had arrived there before the Russians arrived in the area assigned as the Soviet Zone. The Americans requisitioned Tante Lotti's house at Ludwigslust. They threw her out of her house without her possessions or anywhere else to live, so neighbours took her in for a while. In her house, she had had on display her treasured piece of Meissen china, which she loved. She had bought it on a silver-wedding visit to the porcelain towns of Dresden and Meissen. Unfortunately, the Americans used it for target practice, and they burnt the stair bannisters to fuel the heating boiler. Then, in the first days of July 1945, after two months, the Americans left. Then the English moved in, who allowed Tante Lotti to move back into her house when she learned of the destruction of the porcelain and the missing staircase bannisters that the Americans had destroyed. When the English also moved out of her house, she had to make way for the Russian administration, in accordance with the terms of the treaty signed at Yalta.

Tante Lotti described how her house at Ludwigslust was completely taken over by Russians, including a Russian officer and his batman, who moved in but allowed Tante Lotti and Anneliese to stay. The Russians had their own women with them, who cooked for them. Tante Lotti complained when the women used her grand piano as an ironing board and instead provided them with an ironing table. Then, one day, she alerted the batman to the fact that the young lieutenant had been a long time in the bathroom and that she could smell gas. He was discovered collapsed in the bath, overcome by fumes. Fortunately for him, he had pulled the plug out with his toe to let out the water so was not in danger of drowning, but he could have died, had he not been found just in time because the pilot light on the geyser had gone out. After that incident, Tante Lotti was treated with courtesy because she had saved the man's life. The Russians even gave food to her and Anneliese because this had put them on good terms with the Russians. Charlotte learned that, during the occupation era, her Aunt Lotti had hidden family silver for safety in the garden. It may have included the special silver ladle that Charlotte had inherited from her but had not received. Maybe it remains there to this day. Who knows? It would be some years before she would gain permission to visit the aunts she loved.

Holidays Abroad

In 1948, about one year after they were married, Charlotte and Michael began a holiday, which included a visit to Paris. Because they were only allowed to take £25 spending money, they travelled slowly, staying at youth hostels, which were very good and cheap. Members could pay in advance in their own countries. One of the hostels was a chalet in Brunnen, Switzerland, which Charlotte said was lovely. The food was good, and they were provided with sandwiches for lunch. The simple bedrooms had single beds with nice Gingham bed linen and had beautiful views of the mountains. Because they had so little money, they could only look at the delicious cream cakes and buns in the shop windows. They regarded this holiday as a sort of honeymoon. Anyone connected with Hitler was unpopular, so it was best not to say that she was German.

Michael had arranged for them to stay on the way to Switzerland with a Parisian family at their summer residence at Vernon on the River Seine. Michael had explained that it was the family to whom he had been allocated during the war following the D-Day landings, while he was in military accommodation. Michael had explained to Charlotte how he and the other Sappers of his unit were allocated to French families for hospitality and were sent in various directions as part of the programme to help reconstruction. But Charlotte learned that she had not been put fully in the picture when she learned something that made her feel embarrassed. Michael had not told her in advance that he and Janine, the daughter of the family, had had a bit of a romance. Charlotte said she would never have agreed to stay there if she had known about it. It is not something she likes to recall. But later, she told me she is or was tickled to think of this romance of Michael's. She added that the daughter was only a young girl.

Although it was such a short time between her last holiday with Manfred, in March 1945, and then getting to know Michael, she said they seemed part of two completely separate worlds, which, of course, they were. But Manfred would stay in her memory forever.

A Holiday in the Black Forest

When Charlotte visited Freiburg, while on holiday in Europe with Michael, she discovered, when she searched discreetly in the telephone directory, that Manfred's telephone number was recorded there, and it appeared that he had survived the war. This was a relatively short time after she had last said goodbye to him when she got on the train at Freiburg early in 1945. Charlotte then had to make a very difficult decision as to whether she should contact Manfred. She decided that it was best not to do so, although she was sorely tempted. However, she thought she shouldn't because she was married. She could not see the sense in it and hid her sadness from Michael, whom she did not tell about Manfred. She said she did not discuss Manfred with Michael. She said he never showed an interest in him, but he was aware of him in the background. But significantly, Charlotte kept all her life the copy she had made of Manfred's telephone number. I was taken by surprise when she mentioned, shortly after Michael died in 2021, when she was aged 94, that she had sought out the phone number again, and it appears that a Manfred Kurz was still in the directory.

Charlotte is also curious to know what happened to the helpful submarine officer who had been so kind. She so valued his help of carrying her suitcase during the perilous walk on her journey home from seeing Manfred in the Erzgebirge Mountains.

On one of their visits to Germany, Charlotte and Michael they stayed overnight at the Stift Bethlehem hospital in Ludwigslust, possibly in 1953. Next morning at breakfast, when Charlotte looked up from the dining table, she saw a portrait of her great uncle looking down at her.

To Huntingdonshire

Charlotte and Michael left Birmingham for Michael's new job at the Ministry of Works at Wyton Aerodrome in Huntingdonshire.

They stayed for a week at the George Hotel in Huntingdon, but it was expensive, so they began the search for somewhere to rent.

Charlotte, by that time, was very experienced at searching for new places to live. She approached someone in Huntingdon High Street and told her she was looking for accommodation. She learned from that person of a German lady who was married to an Englishman, who lived on the same road as her at Hartford. Charlotte visited the address at Hartford and explained she and Michael were looking for rooms. The couple were friendly and welcoming and let them have rooms with them. Gisela Tattersall, née Roupell, who was from Frankfurt, had come to England as an au pair where she met her husband Edward, who was known as Tat. During the war, her husband had been sent to Egypt, and Gisela became a Land Army girl in England while her German brother was fighting in Russia. The couple were glad to have the company of Charlotte and Michael. They already had a cleaner, but Charlotte shared the cooking.

To get to work, Michael had to cycle up the long, very steep hill to the aerodrome at Wyton but then, after work, would fly down it at speed. Charlotte used to meet him halfway home and watched as he rode down with his coat billowing out behind him.

On one occasion, the Tattersalls left their children in Michael and Charlotte's care to stay at The Brown Teapot, a tearoom and bed and breakfast in Houghton village. This was to allow the Tattersalls to have some time to themselves because they had been parted while he was serving in

Egypt and had not had a honeymoon. Charlotte, who had had much experience of looking after children in her Pflicht year, described how Michael was clumsy and managed to spill the teaspoonful of sticky orange juice over the little one's pram covers. She said it was like having three children to look after. The two couples became close friends and holidayed together. Because the youngest of the children was only a baby, Mrs Tattersall came back in the evening from the Brown Teapot in Houghton to see him.

Charlotte said, because Michael was beginning to be a pacifist, he left Wyton for a job as a quantity surveyor for the County Council, but he then took a job as a quantity surveyor for the building firm of Mr Brudenell because it offered accommodation. They moved into one of Mr Brudenell's houses in Linden Grove, Godmanchester. Michael's skills made possible the successful expansion of the Godmanchester building firm, where Michael did the estimating for the builder. Charlotte considered Michael ought to receive a higher salary and told him to ask Mr Brudenell for a rise. She said that, when Michael returned home without doing so, she would not let him into the house until he did ask. I am not sure if that is quite correct. After the request for a higher salary was turned down, Charlotte persuaded a reluctant Michael that it made sense for him to set up his own business as an independent quantity surveyor.

Charlotte said Michael's first step was to send out letters to say he was setting up on his own. He created the successful firm of Fellows & Ballard at 37 High Street, Huntingdon. Michael's business thrived because he used the same skills he had used when working for Mr Brudenell, where he had been good at dealing with architects and builders. His former employer's business did not do as well because Michael's replacement was not as good at surveying or at public relations. Michael was good at making relationships and engaging with those in the building trade during his everyday work and knew the price of such things as nails. He would keep in touch with people and remind them of decisions.

On 10 September 1952, Charlotte's first baby, Susan, was born at Paxton Hall, which had been converted into a maternity hospital. Two more daughters followed, named Helen and Michelle.

Figure 41 Merryweather

Figure 42 Charlotte and Michael at Merryweather

After exploring the area on their bikes, Charlotte and Michael decided Hemingford Abbots, which was situated not far from Godmanchester, was where they would like to live. Eighteen months later, they bought two adjacent building plots in Common Lane from Mr Smith, the farmer at Home

Farm, and had a house designed and built to their requirements, naming it Merryweather. 60 years ago, the house was opposite the plot the Caldwells had chosen for their house. Because they had no car, Charlotte used to cycle to the shops in St Ives and discovered, on the return journey along Common Lane to Merryweather, that it was up what was considered to be a hill in the very flat landscape. Because the house was a way up Common Lane, Charlotte did not at first join in village activities, but that was not for long. After 30 years at Merryweather, Charlotte and Michael left it to retire to a house nearby that they had had designed and built in Abbots Close. Merryweather was demolished in about 1983 and replaced by a house at least double the size covering the former two plots to become no. 43 Common Lane. Coincidently, the house built opposite Merryweather by the Caldwells has also been demolished and replaced by a larger and more up-to-date architectural style. This is a common experience in the constantly changing landscape of once rural Hemingford Abbots.

Daily Life for Charlotte's Aunts under the Soviet Regime

In 1956, after much time and effort trying to get permission to visit her aunts in Mecklenburg in the Soviet Zone, Charlotte finally got a permit. This was about the time of the Hungarian revolution, which occurred in 1956 between 23 October and 10 November and which was ruthlessly put down. In spite of the dangerous situation, Charlotte decided that, because it had taken so long to get a permit, they should take the risk and travel into the Russian Zone. She says she didn't care about the Russians. When they arrived in Hamburg at the time of the Hungarian uprising, Charlotte and Michael, with 4-year-old Susan, were not allowed to take their car through border control. They had to report at Hamburg station, and their visit was to be supervised. A Russian observer met them, and they were followed by him and had to register everywhere to let the Russians know where they were going.

Charlotte, Michael, and daughter Susan had caught a train on the Hamburg to Berlin railway to stay in a B & B in Ludwigslust.

When they visited Tante Lotti and Tante Leni, who were living under Stalin's regime, they experienced Stalin's communist propaganda in the form of huge distracting placards and noisy loud speakers, which were played throughout the day and were so loud that she asked her aunts how they could put up with it. They said they grew to ignore it. Because they were used to experiencing Hitler's propaganda, they didn't listen. Charlotte said she thought the communist form of propaganda was worse than Hitler's. In the schools, Russian became the second language and the way of life there was very different from that experienced in West Germany. There were Russian soldiers everywhere. Charlotte said that, though it has since become part of Germany, the way of life has not caught up yet.

They discovered that Tante Lotti was living in very much changed circumstances. The Russians had left by then, but Charlotte was upset to find the luxurious home of her aunt and adopted daughter Anneliese had been divided into homes for three families. They were sharing a small kitchen with two other families and had only two rooms for themselves. The rooms had been subdivided with hardboard that did not reach the ceiling. The luxurious carpets and furnishing of the middle-class home had gone. It looked horrible. The families sharing Tante Lotti's home were East Prussian refugees, whose land had been given away to Soviet Russia. The situation had to be accepted. They had no choice.

Tante Leni's nephew, Charlotte's cousin, Dieter Krabbe, picked them up from Tate Lotti's to take them to Tante Leni's home in Schwerin. They discovered that, in spite of living under Soviet rule, Tante Leni was fortunate to be able to continue to live in her nice two-bedroomed flat, with its dining and sitting room. It was on the top floor of a block of flats. It would be the last time that Charlotte would see Tante Leni. She mentioned that Tante Leni did not make a will and that she feels sad about this as she has no memento of her aunt and their life together. She feels that someone could have thought to save her a small item. Another source of sadness for Charlotte is the loss of a very detailed family tree of both the Krabbe and the Dabelstein families, which Tante Leni had diligently constructed.

We can see that, as soon as the war ended, with Germany's surrender, Tante Lotti had been forced to accept a complete change to her once very comfortable standard of living, which included a housekeeper and a maid. Her life would never be the same again. This was another example of the legacy of Hitler and the Nazis and was very far from making Germans the superior race. Under the Soviet regime, Tante Lotti had no income, but she received some payment from the refugee tenants who now shared the house, which they would eventually own. This enabled her to live in the house without paying rent as long as she lived. English newspapers were banned, but Charlotte had managed to hang onto a copy of *The Observer*, which she had bought on the station at Hamburg to give to her aunt. She said that surprisingly she did manage to read it openly when travelling on the train to Tante Lotti's, although the population in East Germany was forbidden by the Russians to read such newspapers. Tante Lotti was pleased to see Charlotte and delighted to receive the English newspaper. She was so keen to read the news that Charlotte translated it into German for her.

On a later visit to see Tante Lotti, Charlotte found her much-loved aunt very thin and permanently bedridden because she was suffering from liver cancer. She was being cared for by her adopted daughter Anneliese and her grandson Robert and was also receiving care from the refugees who looked after her and cleaned the house. In later years, grandson Robert became a teacher. After his marriage, he gave his older brother Herbert (the second baby of Anneliese) a home because Herbert had had an unfortunate history and had been in trouble. Robert had grown up to be a very caring person.

On a further visit to Aunt Lotti's former home, possibly in the 1960s, Charlotte found it had new occupants. She was only allowed to look into the back entrance. The big hall, where Jürgen had been allowed to have young people for parties, was neglected. This was the house that her uncle and aunt had built for themselves. The big cellar underneath had a window, but all seemed horrible. It was run down, and the paintwork was blistering. There had been no repairs during the war or afterwards. She missed the large oak tree that she had once admired because it had screened the view from the house in earlier times, but it was now gone. It had had to be cut down when it became dangerous. There was no indication that there had ever been soft fruit or morello cherries growing up the wall. The plants were dead. Charlotte found it hard to accept that everything had changed so much in what seemed such a relatively short time.

Charlotte's Projects

I have mentioned that Charlotte did not consider life in England an anti-climax. She said that the effort of learning to speak English was part of the reason for that, but she had also busied herself with several projects that would make a difference to her own and to other people's lives.

She described how she became a civil servant in Huntingdon, where she worked as assistant officer to Hostels Officer Mr Horner at the War Rural Agriculture Department. There, she dealt with ex-POWs, displaced persons of different nationalities, but mainly Germans who could not go home to their parts of Germany where they would no longer be welcome. Charlotte said there was not much work for her to do. She visited St Peter's in Huntingdon, Buckden, Ramsey, Warboys, and Yaxley, which were the five camps in Huntingdonshire. She said the camps were hostels rather than camps, consisting of huts. Some were Nissen huts. She said she addressed any complaints made by the displaced people. They organized themselves and chose a mentor from among them. She checked the bills of each camp. They had separate bills, so she instigated centralized buying from one butcher to be more efficient. This was unpopular. She remarked that the Germans probably got less meat this way but that it saved the Government money. She arranged for the rations to be shared more fairly when she became aware that, where the allowance was handed to one person, that person gave himself a larger share and ate better quality meat than the others. She reprimanded one person because of this.

Making a Difference

It was while doing this work that she came in contact with the Quakers, who were checking up on the welfare of those in the camps. The Quakers needed permission to visit the POWs to see what they needed in order to help them. This contact with the Quakers led to Charlotte and Michael's lives taking on a new focus. They attended a meeting of the Huntingdon Quakers that was held in the home of a couple of its members. Because it was in a small room in a private house it could not be labelled a meeting house. This limited the size of the membership. The couple objected to the proposed idea that the meetings should move out of their home to bigger premises to overcome the problem. They wished meetings to continue in their home, so discontent simmered. Charlotte and Michael were among those who left to attend a meeting house in Jesus Lane, Cambridge. Once the discontent simmered down, a search began for suitable premises for a Friends' meeting house, but the search was unsuccessful as all properties and land were too expensive. However, the run-down Rose and Crown public house, with attached dwelling house, was seen to offer a possible solution. The building, which had been empty for some time, parts of which dated from different centuries, presented quite an undertaking. Money continued to be raised to cover the considerable costs while the work was going on. Charlotte and Michael became guarantors and were responsible for building it as a meeting house. An appeal for money was made to all the other meeting houses, and all contributed. Contributions came from all over the world, most of which were from Great Britain. They managed to pay off the debt in 2 years. An architect named Dennis Adams designed its conversion to a meeting house while Michael priced the work. Charlotte explained that there was a smell of alcohol present, and very smelly urinals had to be pulled down. Michael was responsible for the rebuilding of the living house as a separate entity.

The result of all the effort was the Rose and Crown Public Quaker Centre, 48 Post Street, Godmanchester. It provided a place of worship and space for other groups, including a nursery. It is a Grade-II listed building and Heritage Centre.

Today, Charlotte is still in contact with members of the Society of Friends (Quakers), who meet occasionally at her house.

Another of Charlotte's projects was the setting up of a Cambridge group of the 'Samaritans'. She gave up her role in the Samaritans only when the system changed to include having to do night duty. This was not convenient for her.

She said her proudest achievement was that she set up the Citizens Advice Bureau (CAB) in Huntingdon. She said Michael had some influence on this through his contacts in the Rotary Club and the District Council. The bureau was located in the former gas showroom in Huntingdon and was manned by advisers and specialists such as solicitors, who gave free advice to people with problems. She said questions were often to do with accommodation. If they did not know the answers, the CAB searched for them. Once the Bureau was well underway, a manager took Charlotte's place, leaving her free to use her energies and talents elsewhere.

Another project, which she set in motion with a friend in 1984, was the monthly village lunch club. It was held in Hemingford Abbots village hall for men and women. In spite of the first lunch being poorly attended, it has proved to be an important feature of Hemingford Abbots village community. It continued non-stop until the advent of the coronavirus pandemic but has resumed. Diners are on a rota, with teams taking it in turn to provide the meal for everyone to share and meet in a friendly atmosphere. It has become a village tradition as has the summertime lunch held in John and Anne Sink's garden in Common Lane in July, and a Christmas lunch held in the village hall in December. Both are popular and well attended.

Danger in Peacetime

But, unlikely as it may seem, Charlotte also encountered dangers in postwar England although she was not in a war zone. In her newly built house, a newly installed gas appliance proved to be a danger. One day, when Charlotte was at home in Merryweather with her young daughter Michelle, she became aware that the pilot light of the central heating had gone out. Unbeknown to her, gas was escaping into the room. When she lit a match and bent to relight it, it exploded in her face, and she found herself across the room by the French windows. Her hair and face were burned, as were her hands where she had tried to extinguish the flames. She escaped through the French window with her hair alight, whilst trying to pat it out. Her neighbour took her to the A & E department at the hospital, while her friend Donna took care of Michelle, who fortunately had been in a safe place in a baby chair. Later, when Charlotte inspected the carpet, she saw there were scorch marks showing the outline of her feet. She had had another very lucky escape. The family decided not to pursue the firm that had installed the appliance.

She had yet another lucky escape when approaching Huntingdon bridge in a stop-start queue of traffic. An impatient woman in the car behind hers drove into the back of her. Charlotte was propelled forward and hit her face on the steering wheel, causing her to visit the hospital and have stitches put in her face.

Further Projects

Charlotte took on another public-spirited role by becoming a visitor to Littlehay Prison near Huntingdon, which was for men with long-term convictions for sex offences. Charlotte found the role unsatisfactory in many ways. It was an unpleasant experience, which she did not enjoy, partly because it was a long drive to the prison, where she had to wait a considerable time for the entrance to be unlocked. On arrival, the visitors were kept waiting in a cage and allocated one specific person to look after who had been convicted of sexual misdemeanours. They were prisoners who had no one to visit them. The first chaplain, when she was there, was not good, and she could not get on with him. He had no sympathy for the prisoners and did not help them, although they were there for re-education. She said his heart was not in it. The situation was not helpful for the prisoners' rehabilitation in other ways. The prison warden had to accompany the visitor, so conversations were not confidential, and also the prisoners kept being moved from one prison to another. There was no sense of continuity. Charlotte decided it was not something she could help with.

Charlotte grew up among a supportive extended family network, whose members she did not consider to be Nazis, except perhaps for one member, who was not much to her liking. He was an uncle who was a Nazi German officer at Narvik in Norway. He was the sort of person who liked to give orders. He had fought in WWI. Charlotte has now explained that her uncle Hans-Hugo, who was an officer in charge of the Battle of Narvik in the Arctic Circle in Norway, was not a Nazi, but she did not like him. He was arrogant, with a forceful nature, and was not a likeable type of person. She mentioned an example of his character, which occurred when Tante Lotti had arranged to see him. It was when the troops were passing through Ludwigslust by train on the route between Hamburg and Berlin. Charlotte was present. She said the troops were being moved from one place to another. Her uncle managed to visit Tante Lotti for half an hour. She had managed, through her relationship with local shopkeepers, to acquire ingredients to bake a cake containing raisins to give to him. But when she offered it to her brother, Hans-Hugo, he refused her offering, saying he did not like raisins. Charlotte felt he should not have let her aunt know he didn't want it because she had done a kind thing when food was scarce.

We now return to Charlotte's close friend Edith, whom she last saw close to the end of the war when visiting the dentist in Parchim in Mecklenburg in 1945. On that occasion, she had bumped into Edith entirely by chance and urged her to escape from her work camp because the Russians were approaching. It was only during a postwar visit to Europe with Michael that she once again met her school friend, also by chance. They bumped into each other in a street in Bad Oeynhausen, Lower Saxony. Only then did Charlotte learn whether Edith had acted on her warning that she was in danger and that she must escape from her work camp immediately.

Charlotte now learned that Edith had taken her advice and had rushed back to her unit, where she packed a small bag with the barest minimum of items, so as not to arouse the suspicions of those who would have stopped her from leaving. She then set off for her home in Hanover, some miles away. She told Charlotte how she had travelled all the way on foot, following railway tracks because road traffic signs had been removed. Starting at 8.00 a.m. each day, she walked until 5.00 pm each evening, when she would throw herself on people's mercy. She knocked on people's doors, asking if she could have a bed for the night. On at least one occasion, she had to sleep in a barn. She might have been given something to eat in the morning, but people had little food for themselves, apart from perhaps in the countryside where there may have been a little. Edith had her ration card with her but had to rely on strangers' kindness. Fortunately, Hanover was situated in the English zone, so once there, she was safely out of reach of the Russians.

It took Edith six weeks to get home. When her family had not heard from her during that time, they thought she must be dead until someone from her village, who was cycling further away, saw Edith as she was heading home. Because her family home had been bombed during one of the many bombing raids on Hanover, she aimed for the small village where her mother now lived with other family members. The cyclist who had seen her had raced back to them to give her mother the good news that Edith was safe and she was met on her arrival with great rejoicing. A very grateful Edith kept in touch with Charlotte until she died, possibly in 2020. She had married and lived in Hamburg. She was so grateful to Charlotte for the rest of her life because without Charlotte's warning she would not have realized that the Russians were only a short distance from the work camp where she had been working. Without Charlotte's advice, she might not have had the courage to attempt to escape because of possible retribution. Charlotte, when considering Edith's journey in retrospect, is perplexed as to why Edith's journey took so long. She wonders what obstacles had delayed her. She learned that with the ending of the war, Edith was able to go to university as she had intended. Following their reunion in Bad Oeynhausen, Charlotte and Edith took a holiday together during the year of the floods. Although warning signs said the roads were closed and people were ordered not to go, Charlotte chose to ignore the flood warnings. She said they managed to drive through the not very deep water outside the Lüneburg Heath because the road was higher than the floods.

On one occasion, they visited the Baltic, an inland sea, which has little salt and lovely white sand. It is a safe area for bathing.

Charlotte said she took two holidays each year, including a visit to Europe. It was during one of the holidays in Germany with Edith, that Charlotte saw a signpost pointing to her grandfather Theodor Martin Krabbe's parsonage, where she knew he was buried.

Visit to Banzin

Many years after the war, when travelling on the Hamburg and Berlin railway, she returned to visit the Farm at Banzin. An event happened that she finds hard to accept to this day. She had only identified the former farm's location because of a sign with the name Banzin on it, but to her great shock there was hardly anything to indicate that Banzin had ever existed. Charlotte's belongings, including her cherished books and photographs, which she had left in the storeroom of the farm when she escaped, had all gone. She so regrets not keeping some photos with her. In particular, one her father, who was a keen photographer, had taken on his Leica camera of her on her favourite swan rocking chair with its two handles on its neck. Andreas often used her as a model. Of the main house, which had been like a small castle, only part of a wing of the white-stuccoed main house remained, in which strangers were living. She saw someone emptying a bin. She is not sure whether they were German-speaking refugees or squatters. They knew nothing of the farm's previous existence.

There was no sign that the farmhouse, in which Charlotte had lived and worked and which had been her home for 18 months, had ever existed except for some abandoned house bricks. The whole farm with its associated buildings and stables had gone. It had totally disappeared into a landscape of overgrown heathland. Gone were the crops, which had included the sugar beet from which the farm had made their own sugar. Gone were the familiar faces, including those of the owners of the house, the farmer's family, the various foreign workers, refugees, and prisoners, including one named Radic. All was gone, and there was no indication of what had happened to them. Charlotte says she can't get over it and that she was shaken by it. She finds it hard to comprehend even now. because of what she did not find on that visit, Charlotte realizes she had made the right decision to leave when the Russians were approaching because it appears that the farm had been the site of a battle. The forester's house in the forest, where she had stayed, had also disappeared and with it, the few personal items she had left there before having to escape. She thinks the whole area must have been fought over. But she still today feels a sense of shock, and she wondered whether her life there had been a mirage or a mere figment of her imagination, until she discovered Radic, one person, who had definitely not been imagined. She counts it as a significant end to an important part of her life.

After this visit, Charlotte was on another holiday, sightseeing in Yugoslavia, during the time when Marshall Tito was Prime Minister (1944 –63), President for life (1953–80), and Chief Architect of the Socialist Federal Republic of Yugoslavia. To her amazement, Charlotte thought she recognized someone there, and he recognized her too and confirmed he was Radic. He was one of the Yugoslavian POWs whom she had known at the farm at Banzin. She spoke to him only briefly because she was so surprised to see him. She did not think to ask about what he had experienced when the Russians arrived. She only learned that he was a farm labourer. But seemingly, he had managed to leave Banzin unscathed.

Postwar Eastern Germany

In later postwar years Charlotte visited the Bergen-Belsen museum in the heathland. She was shocked because it seemed to her that the true horrors were not portrayed sufficiently graphically for people to grasp the magnitude of the wickedness and cruel treatment of the victims and that they would not get a true experience of the ill treatment and cruelty that had taken place in that concentration camp. The English burnt down the buildings immediately after arriving because of the danger of disease.

After her marriage, Charlotte was in contact with her stepmother Erna once again. She had made peace with her, although she considered she was not a nice person. Among the precious items from her former family home in Hanover that were given to her were the diaries written by Andreas when he was a POW. They were a very welcome surprise. Charlotte also gained a six-person silver cutlery set, which she had inherited from her mother plus a silver tea set and a portrait of her grandfather.

Michael and their children Susan, Helen, and Michelle got to know step grandmother Erna and her son Klaus over long weekends, including during visits to the Fellows' family holiday cottage at Overstrand in Norfolk. Later, Erna, who had been well protected by insurance taken out by Andreas, was able to go into a nice home for old people where Charlotte visited her. Charlotte felt a sense of relief when

Erna died because she had found the relationship difficult to continue.

The Wartime Romance

Manfred and Charlotte were from different backgrounds and from very different parts of Germany, with different customs and culture. Religion does not seem to have played a part in their relationship although Charlotte was from the Protestant North and Manfred from a Roman Catholic area. If they had stayed together, it might have been a problem in the future. He was an officer in the Germany army, with a 1st-class Iron Cross. It is possible he might have expected his wife to be a more conventional housewife if they had married. He was her choice over some other possible boyfriends whom she might have chosen while growing up. She said she had rejected one boy who wished her to be his girlfriend and she would not even be his penfriend. In the end, it was Michael who would be her true romance.

Figure 43 Michael wearing his Légion d'honneur medal

Michael died of dementia in a care home in 2021. Although their daughters may have thought it was a blessing, Charlotte said she misses him and is weepy. But, on my visit to her on 6 August 2021, to my great surprise, she said she had looked to see if Manfred was still alive, even though he was three years older than her and probably aged 97. She discovered that his address was still there in the directory.

Enduring Friendships

Among her enduring friendships was her close friend Barbara Langen née Lorenz. Their friendship began whilst they were pupils at Ludwigslust School and was resumed in Hanover in 1945 when Barbara fortuitously turned up at the officers' mess.

It continued for many years. In the 1960s, Charlotte and Michael travelled through Germany and Denmark to visit

Charlotte's uncle's family in Sweden. On their way, they left Susan, their 16-year-old daughter, in Hamburg with Barbara to learn German for her German language exam. Barbara had moved there from Ludwigslust to marry a widower, who already had children. Barbara was Charlotte's best friend, and her daughters Susan, Helen, and Michelle were fond of her and used the nickname Bärbel for her.

Merigart was another lifelong friend. They had been very close from early days when they were children at school in Hanover.

Edith was yet another lifelong friend of Charlotte's. They had been friends from her early days at the elementary school in Hanover and continued until Edith died.

Some of those running the concentration camps had to face trial at Nuremburg and were executed for their crimes. The British detained Himmler after he attempted to escape after the surrender, but he managed to escape by committing suicide by cyanide poisoning on 23 May 1945.

But Hitler's legacy was a ruined Germany and millions of lost lives and, more importantly for Charlotte, the loss of her beloved brother Jürgen.

Printed in Great Britain
by Amazon